No. 5- A 499 T

JOHN W. MACKAY

"a reticent, soft-spoken and uncommonly able Irishman who carried his blankets up the steep trails to Virginia City in 1859 and left the town some eigh~~~~~~~~~~ter in an ornate Virginia and Tru~~~~~~~~~~~~~~~~~aire.

ROCKE~~~~~~~~~~~~~~~~~~~~

is assured a high place among chronicles of the American West."

Visalia Times Delta

"Rocket of the Comstock is a fascinating account of one of Nevada's most colorful eras . . . when Paiute and Civil wars dominated the political scene, and at home a mule could drop through the ceiling. Plumbago brought on cramps, but arsenic was considered beautifying for the complexion. In this crowded, unpretentious society, a man was accepted for what he was really worth. And Mackay was king.

"Well written and well documented. Mrs. Tomes has mined the Comstock and come up with treasure."

Los Angeles Times

A COMSTOCK EDITION

ROCKET
of the
COMSTOCK

(The Story of John William Mackay)

Ethel Van Vick Tomes

BALLANTINE BOOKS—NEW YORK

BALLANTINE BOOKS, INC.
201 East 50th Street, New York, N.Y. 10022

To
My Wonderful
Mother

ACKNOWLEDGMENTS

In collecting material for this book, I called upon so many people for assistance that it is impossible to list all of those to whom I am obligated. I am especially indebted to Mr. Frank Brezee and other members of the staff of the Bancroft Library, University of California at Berkeley; Mr. Henry Gossie of Reno, Nevada; Mr. Clarence Mackay of New York City; Mrs. Lottie Barnum of Virginia City, Nevada; State Librarian E. Chas. D. Marriage of the Nevada State Library, Carson City; Miss Jeanne Elizabeth Wier of the Nevada State Historical Society, Reno; Miss Caroline Wenzel of the California State Library, Sacramento; Mr. B. W. Coleman, Chief Justice of the Supreme Court of Nevada; Mr. Austin E. Hutcheson, Department of History and Political Science, University of Nevada, Reno; Miss Mabel W. Thomas, Chief Reference Librarian of the Oakland Public Library, Oakland, California; the staff of the Sutro Branch of the California State Library, San Francisco; the staff of the San Francisco Public Library; Mr. Thomas Lewis, Manager of the *Los Angeles Times* News Bureau; Miss Helen E. Wright of the *Oakland Tribune;* Mr. John W. Finch, Director of the Bureau of Mines, United States Department of the Interior, Washington, D.C.; The United States Geological Survey, Department of the Interior; Mr. T. D. Quinn, Administrative Assistant to the Attorney General, Department of Justice, Washington, D.C.; Mrs. Christine Behrman, Placerville, California; Mr. W. H. Goldsworthy of Berkeley; and countless pioneers of Virginia City, Carson City, and Reno.

Table of Contents

I	Washoe Contour	1
II	Parallels	10
III	Springboard to Fortune	19
IV	Letting Out the Tucks	29
V	Immeasurable Empire	43
VI	Refocusing the Lens	61
VII	"Sand" of Flesh and Blood	74
VIII	An Artificial Big Bonanza	81
IX	Evasion and Escape	92
X	Tongues on Wheels	102
XI	President and King	120
XII	Back Stairs' Influence	131
XIII	A New Round	138
XIV	The Big Kindergarten	143
XV	Attempt at Assassination	157
XVI	The Crown Is Removed	164
XVII	Echoes	171
	Footnotes	177

1   Washoe Contour

1

The first thaw of the spring of 1860 was like a charge of dynamite in setting off the second infectious and unorganized rush of adventurers to Utah Territory. Up through the woodland wealth of the California Sierra strode John William Mackay, pack on his back, intent upon being one of the first to reach Washoe with its fabulous Comstock Lode of silver and gold. He had hurriedly closed up his cabin at Smith's Flat on Kentucky Creek to set a grueling pace for Jack O'Brien, young miner who had shared his loaf of sour-dough bread and pot of molasses-sweetened coffee.

They took only three days from the Yuba River to the shores of Lake Tahoe—a sapphire-like jewel that shone palely beside the creations of their fired imaginations. Here they were joined by straining, unwashed hikers from Placerville. Blockades of snow had called an unexpected halt to the advance of hundreds of heavily loaded freighters bound for Gold Hill and Virginia City, mining camps beyond Carson City.

Burros laden with blankets, tools, and food, formed swaying pack trains jostled this pair from Alleghany, Sierra County, California, and vied with them for possession of the narrow trail. Pale and tired cityfolk cast envious glances at the ruddy-complexioned twins who lengthened their step in passing. These mustached Irish were no small part of the new movement. Their energy and persistence were what the great lode demanded.

It took them three more days from the crest of California to the distant Washoe range. John Mackay's eyes narrowed as he studied the peculiar arrangement of peaks, each one

1

scarified by ugly gaps, their jowls eroded and pinched together into scraggy, waterless canyons. Here nature had stacked her mountains as a gambler stacks his cards—to all appearances quite carelessly, but doubtless with scheming purpose. Was this to be another game of faro, with one chance in thousands of winning? He thought not. The ragged forbidding sheaf of mountains before him would, in truth, offer a struggle for a type of supremacy unknown to the world. At Washoe would transpire no miracle, but a pitched battle in an underground gymnasium between men with hearts of oak.

John Mackay had not sideslipped into mining as so many thousands had. He did not burrow into the earth and scratch the gravel along the rivers as a temporary means of earning a living the way carefree Jack O'Brien did. Mining was his career, his future, his fortune in the making! Though the Yuba had given him little encouragement, this intrepid fellow had refused to abandon mining, and he actually expanded in confidence with added obstacles. If pluck and fortitude were the stepping stones to mining wealth, if this were to be a struggle among only stout hearts, Mackay believed he could match the best.

Little did this fighting cock realize that even then the mains were being prepared for a giant contest. He was to be pitted against not one but a score of equally stubborn champions whose spurs had been sharpened likewise on the grindstones of the Sierra ranges.

Young Mackay shifted his blankets to the opposite shoulder and urged Jack on through alternating snow and rain. The precipitous grades of the eastern slopes receded as the two men continued to the valley of the Carson. Crossing its level ground, they reached Devil's Gate at the base of Gold Canyon. A mile beyond its misshapen camp of Gold Hill, and two thousand feet above the Carson River, was Virginia City, terrified infant hanging determinedly to the eastern hem of Sun Mountain. This peak, sixteen hundred feet above the town, was the highest mount in the surrounding lumpy ridge of drab brown rocks. It had already been renamed Mount Davidson in honor of a San Francisco banker who had bought a consignment of Washoe's first ore. Across its sides clambered an assortment of human types such as no mountain had ever seen before. Through its substructure ran the huge quartz vein, the Comstock Lode, where nature had kneaded into the unprolific clay her most precious metals.

Mackay smiled. Surely the reports of the wealth of this region had been exaggerated. Two hundred and seventy-five thousand dollars was the total yield for 1859. The leading mines—Ophir, Central, Bowers, and Plato—were said to be employing but ten miners each.

He had left Alleghany for this lopsided camp, located upon the most unnatural spot for a city in all America. Sixteen miles northeast of Carson City, its ridiculous nests of flimsy huts managed to cling to the barren mountainside only with the aid of numerous perpendicular props. Here nothing vegetable grew except the obstinate sage with its persistent yellow flowers. The few stunted cedars and pines, which earlier had formed small groves along the canyons, had been cleared during the past winter to shelter and warm the freezing population. Piñon and juniper had gone up in the smoke of miners' fires; all underbrush had been fed to the starving beasts of that first migration.

It was apparent to John Mackay that every bit of wood for future houses, fuel, and timbering of the mines must come from the mantle of the Sierra. Roads, instead of trails, would have to be blasted through the rocks so that large supplies of food and clothing might be transported from California to the growing camp. Even water, most important of all necessities, would have to be piped from a great distance. The melting snows, which then formed dubious streams in Washoe's canyons, would soon disappear in the pores of the parched ravines. Here was a region that demanded all the energy of which young America boasted, a spot where life itself must be imported. Yet in spite of its barrenness, Mackay felt its compelling attraction and its elusive promise.

The main rivers of the area flowed inward toward a common point and lost themselves within a radius of seventy-five miles. To the south was a desert of acrid sage through which the Carson River meandered in a northeasterly direction until it disappeared in its alkaline sink beyond. Still farther south the washboard contours of the Pine Nut Range overlooked the Walker River as it followed a tortuous course to a brackish burial ground between the Wassuk and Gabbs Valley ranges. From the northeast zig-zagged the Humboldt River, until it became lost by deep percolation in a basin of gloom. Only the Truckee River, springing from Lake Tahoe, moved with speed and purpose in its rapid descent through a series of valleys; but it came to a dead end in shrinking Pyramid Lake, a thirty-mile-long body of water with no outlet.

Mackay was content that he had not joined the great migration to the silver slopes in July of 1859 when the first breathless race for Washoe began. "It will take a heavy lump of gold for a fling at Washoe silver," he told himself. If he intended to woo Sun Peak with its thousands of suitors, he must be more than clever; and he must be patient.

2

When John Mackay entered the camp of Virginia, the miners were just emerging from their winter quarters. Their faces were friendly, as cold and dejection were behind them. Eager and alive for the first time in months, men in red and blue shirts crowded the doorways to watch the newcomers. Even the stoical Chinese gazed with ill-concealed interest at the strapping pair, Mackay and O'Brien, who stepped along to the clatter of their pots and pans. There was no evidence of six-shooters in their belts, or of those dreaded long knives which cut best on pigtails.

Among the unshaven audience Mackay thought he saw many a San Francisco dude who formerly had sported a starched collar and neatly waxed mustache. He had heard that the exodus of the Golden Gate's foremost citizens had almost crippled that city.

What a village Virginia was—only half a dozen stone houses and slightly more than a score of frame buildings, their doors and windows jutting at all angles, their walls striated by the fury of those madcap winds dubbed "Washoe zephyrs" by the miners. Shallow pits—enlarged coyote holes with roof of dirt and board, and pinewood hovels with rusty stovepipe or whisky-barrel chimney—had housed hundreds of men during the winter.

Mackay noticed the reckless haste with which everyone was entering into this industrial pandemonium. His life had been a pattern of diligence and painstaking effort, and it would be hard for him to change. Yet if he intended to outdo these native Americans with their uncontrolled fervor, he too must go like a Washoe whirlwind.

Born in Dublin, Ireland, on November 28, 1831, John Mackay had immigrated to the United States as a steerage passenger in 1840. The death of his father shortly after the family settled in New York City necessitated John's selling newspapers and shining shoes to help support the other three children and his mother.

The boy's brogue, which often piled up in an excited stutter, and his Old World clothes were early cause for painful embarrassment in school, but he soon learned to put his tight, freckled fists to good use, and these helped him out of many a predicament.

An apprenticeship under William H. Webb, builder of fast clipper craft, occupied his teen years. There followed a few months in Louisville, Kentucky, before he was able to earn his passage on one of Webb's ships sailing around the Horn. Arriving in San Francisco late in 1851, he headed for the mountains to join the thousands of other Jasons who had been collecting there since 1849.

The next eight years of simple miner's fare and outdoor labor, first on the American River, then at Downieville and Alleghany in Sierra County on the Yuba, toughened John Mackay's muscles and broadened his naturally robust figure. However, his early soberness and deliberation were not typical of the California placer miner. While his companions haunted Craycroft's seventy-five-foot bar in Downieville, or descended the mountains to San Francisco on frequent drunken sprees, he spent the evenings in his cabin studying English and geology.

Having come to Washoe to win his fortune from the wonder vein, his friends wondered if his caution and attention to mastery of detail would dull him to the possibilities of large and unexpected chances which might demand prompt attention. If he made any money here, would he value his hard-earned dollars too highly when a master gamble was needed?

3

On the hillside above the Ophir mine, Mackay and O'Brien established themselves. There was more of cave than building about their miserable cabin, and Mark Twain could have been describing its brush-and-dirt roof in his story of the tenderfoot who soon changed his mind about things moving slowly in Washoe when a mule dropped through the ceiling. Beneath this doubtful housetop stood two double-decker bunks. Mackay slept in the lower one on the north side, Alexander Kennedy above him. Jack O'Brien and Pat Corbett occupied the south corner in a similar arrangement.

After storing in grub for the quarter—with the added luxury of sugar, onions, and tea—Mackay explored carefully the supposed line of the lode. Where among its hundreds of adits should he begin work?

The ground of the Union mine presented a free and favorable locality for initial speculation, but it would take considerable money to work even a small mine. Mackay decided to seek a financial partner, since Jack O'Brien did not have a cent "in pickle." Elkanah Said was willing to risk his few dollars in a tunnel, so together they began to dig in the abandoned Union ground. The fact that it had been worked the previous year with no success was of no significance to Mackay. The early miners had been anything but systematic; besides, the largest shafts did not extend over fifty feet into the earth. Already John Mackay was choosing a form of reasoning that would determine momentous things in a few years.

As the tunnel lengthened with the days, the patches of fleecy clouds on the ragged skirt of Mount Davidson peeled off one at a time to be whirled away in merry little storms. Before the city below was aware of their departure, the mountain's granite elbows had peeped forth through the rents in its sagebrush jacket.

The spring cloudbursts filled Mackay's tunnel but he did not complain; they sweetened the bitter drinking water. The sun was very bright in the clear, translucent atmosphere.

On May 8, 1860, Washoe rid itself of its spineless members when war with the Piutes began. In retaliation for the mistreatment of two Indian girls by the William brothers, the red men murdered the pair of miscreants and their three guests. Virginia herded its few women and children into Peter O'Riley's new stone house and hastily constructed a fort at Devil's Gate. Major Ormsby led his motley company of regulars in a disastrous charge against Winnemucca, patriarch of the Piutes, who actually was attempting a truce.

Frequently false alarms in the night brought Mackay and his three friends to their feet and rushed them out into the darkness, armed with picks and revolvers, to battle the imaginary invaders. Captain Samuel T. Curtis, miner from the Feather River, raised a group of volunteers in Sacramento and arrived on the lode with a fine supply of weapons and ammunition. Colonel Dan E. Hungerford, acquaintance of Mackay from Downieville, organized the Sierra Guards and raced after Curtis to Washoe. This soldier from New York state, who had won distinction in the Mexican War, was following the profession of barber at the forks of the Yuba in

California for lack of hostilities between nations. Although Hungerford fought against the Piutes in the second battle of Pyramid Lake, the needless war was over before Curtis could prime and load.

Mackay delayed his return to the mine until he was able to see Colonel Hungerford and inquire about the diggings around Downieville. Sierra County was at a standstill, he learned.

"Why don't you move to Virginia?" Mackay asked him.

"Maybe I will. But there's Louisa, and my wife wants to be near her," Hungerford answered.

Mackay recalled that the soldier's attractive daughter had married Dr. Edmund Bryant, a cousin of the poet William Cullen Bryant. She had remained in Downieville while her husband went to answer the urgent call for doctors on the lode.

4

The tent-and-shanty town of Virginia was filling up with speculators, but they weren't the only source of annoyance. By June the polished spring muds of the streets had changed to clouds of choking dust. Loaded with old bonnets, rags, and papers, they whirled through the air at frequent intervals to raise havoc with the pedestrians. Everyone was forced to break for shelter when the dust darkened the streets, some plunging headlong into stores and saloons and others squeezing into doorways. Mackay preferred to brace himself behind a post, his hat pulled low over his eyes, and wait until the fury of the gust had spent itself. With a scarcity of water, the "Old Flying Cloud" sprinkler made only rare appearances.

A clamor for better drinking water arose as goiters began to develop among the townspeople. Though the old-timers insisted that arsenic was beautifying to the complexion, plumbago and other minerals brought on racking cramps.

John Mackay suffered with the rest, and soon followed the example of the old miners in adding "Rifle Whiskey" to water used for drinking purposes. Nothing was going to drive him out.

The summer months, when the sun drew close and Virginia moved like a lazy scorpion, found Mackay and Said swinging pick and shovel in the tunnel, still hoping to strike a thin seam of ore. The arched entrance to their coyote hole was but one of four thousand within a radius of thirty miles, all marking the precipitous sides of Mount Davidson, Six and Seven Mile canyons, Sugar Loaf, and Flowery Ridge.

Mackay's ambitions continued to ride loose-reined and roweled over his doubts and discouragements. He tucked his trousers a little tighter into his boots, pulled his rough felt hat lower over his forehead, and whistled determinedly, "There's a good time coming, boys."

The twinkle began to fade from his eyes, however, as the days shortened and the gigantic columns of whirling sand became raging snowstorms which whitened the basaltic hills and softened the buttes of volcanic ash. The floating population had already departed for California. Times were hard on the barebacked mountains of Washoe. Mackay looked with dismay at his empty purse and holed in as sleet and driving wind brought all work to a standstill. Success was so remote!

The winter of 1860-61 was called a "freeze-out." With the increasing cold, the number of occupants in Mackay's cabin multiplied at an alarming rate. The first addition to the household was instructed to furnish the firewood—no simple task in Washoe. The second man was admitted on condition that he would do the cooking. By Christmas, the shanty sheltered a crowded dozen, the eight newcomers being forced to sleep on the dirt floor, tightly rolled in their coarse blankets.

What did it matter if the snow sifted in and all night long the frosty wind sighed? With lumber three hundred dollars a thousand feet and restaurant meals two dollars each, due to the scarcity of provisions, Virginia's two-thousand-odd persons were grateful for any structure that boasted a stove. Lighthearted Jack O'Brien was still there, and Mackay's deep and enduring affection for him was heart-warming to the other miners.

5

The blizzards of January allowed John Mackay time for sewing on buttons and patching his clothes. When flour sacks gave out, he did some serious figuring. Would it be worth his while to stay here until spring? He had to admit he was discouraged.

Yet he could look upon many improvements in mining made during the past year—the new Washoe process of extracting silver from the matrix, which replaced the ancient arrastra method still used by the Mexican mine; fifteen-horsepower steam engines had replaced the notched poles and hand windlasses formerly used for raising ore and men to the surface; Philipp Deidesheimer's system of square-sets had taken the place of circular supports in most of the shafts—these permitted deeper mining; and the output of bullion had doubled.

It would take time for law and order to smooth the rough edges from Virginia. Most of "the boys" had adopted the habit of carrying revolvers, since everyone was held accountable for his actions. Mackay relied upon his ready fists, telling as loaded muskets, to force at least that outward display of elaborate courtesy so noticeable on the lode. The police were too busy with the "knucks" and "footpads" (thieves and holdup men in Comstock slang) to interfere in personal quarrels.

As Mackay reviewed the fast-shifting scenes of his first year in the mining camp, he observed that a new crop of men had replaced those introductory adventurers—Comstock, Penrod, O'Riley, and McLaughlin. The old floaters had left or become firmly rooted like the scrub pine. Living candidly with his fellow men, a person was accepted for what he was really worth. Here, regardless of education or antecedents, a man of ability could forge ahead.

But the young Irish miner realized that alone he could do nothing. Organization and capital were needed to develop the Comstock Lode. His partnership with Elkanah Said at an end, he sought other alliances. If he could only soar a little, richer panoramas would be deployed before him. Though his circle was small, Mackay knew his horizon was unlimited.

2   Parallels

1

The American flag followed Scotch whiskey and German beer to the twin mining camps, but up to April of 1861 only special celebrations had occasioned its display. Then, just when Washoe was thawing out after a paralyzing winter, a sound other than roaring spring floods reverberated through its swollen canyons. Beating time for the steady scrape of picks came the throb of remote war drums from a land far beyond the campoodies of the Piutes. Mingling with the clatter and crash of the noisy mill stamps sounded the faint notes of distant trumpet and bugle.

"War in the east!" shouted the rider of the Pony Express as he passed through Dayton on the banks of the Carson. Immediately the barren slopes about Mount Davidson—stripped of their pine nut trees, cleared of their pungent sage, and even grubbed of their wandering roots—were swept by the same intense rivalry that found expression in pitched battles amid eastern verdure.

The spring rains were clearing the snow from the dangerous passes of the Sierra. Pack trains from California had already started up the long grade. Make way for more Unionists!—more Secessionists! Plans were begun for the construction of excellent toll roads over the mountains to Placerville. With characteristic enthusiasm for any type of conflict, the miners forgot that a few weeks before they had been starving in ten feet of snow. What did it matter now if the floods were sweeping buildings and valuable stores of grain into the Carson Sink? If the mining shafts in line with the flood filled to the top, they'd pump them dry!

All they considered important was that the fate of a nation

10

was hanging by a thread—a two-strand thread of silver and gold, Washoe's bullion. Their diggings could determine whether North or South would emerge victorious. "Money means half the strength of an army," they told one another as they widened the trails from Virginia to Carson. If ore was to be converted into new coin, they would need better roads to the mint.

John Mackay listened to the heated arguments of the rival factions with the same intentness that had marked his presence at Flood and O'Brien's bar. Treason marched in the ranks of the Washoe army. There were whisperings of a Pacific republic, of the Comstock joining the Confederacy. But "Honest Abe" and "the Union" were words more enduring than "Bonanza." Yearning to be a vital part of young America, Mackay made his choice of party and became a staunch Republican.

However, patriotic fervor alone could not make him forget his purpose in Virginia City. He was here to accumulate a fortune so that his aging mother, whom he was supporting in New York, might return to Dublin for the final years of her life. It was up to him to make her forget those early years of hardship. He told his pal these extravagant dreams, but Jack O'Brien only laughed at him. Where did he get all his notions of fortunes to be kept?

Before activity was general in the mines, Mackay was already tramping the muddy hillsides that lined the windy Divide, descending into wet shafts, and threading his way through damp tunnels.

"If you don't get 'feet' on the lode, it's not due to lack of use of your own legs," his friends teased him as they watched his great piston stride. No, it was a very thin purse that was holding him back. His only course was to work for others and forget the idea of partnerships.

He went the rounds of the mining companies in search of a job and was told that the backward Mexican mine needed workers. The owners of the Mexican company had made money in spite of their wasteful methods in mining. Now they decided to be more systematic, although they still did not adopt the use of square-sets for supporting the tunnels. John Mackay had the reputation of being a hard worker, so they hired him at four dollars a day.

2

With the departing gray tails of wintry clouds, the hills burst into red, yellow, and blue blossoms. It was only the clean dawn that Mackay could enjoy, since his days were spent underground in candlelight, working in the dangerous Mexican mine. Its small crew of miners was removing the black sulphuret vein in reckless haste from the rich ground.

It wasn't long before the men began paying close attention to what John said. Though a quiet fellow, he insisted upon keeping a vigilant eye on the other workers. He cautioned them against removing choice pieces of ore from behind the arrangement of posts and lintels which supported the dirt roof.

"One of those chunks of quartz extracted in the wrong place, and the mountain will come down on your heads. Pass them up!" he ordered brusquely, though he had no authority to do so.

The men progressed more cautiously to avoid a possible cave-in. The tremendous pressure from above was constantly swelling and slackening the ground. Too many of Mackay's friends had lost their lives in these tunnels. He chafed at the miners' inability to penetrate successfully this stubborn mountain. As for himself, he could direct its plundering but not devise new methods for its conquest. Invention was not in his nature.

The summer stages tearing into Virginia were left by the roadside as the outgoing quartz teams took the right of way. Washoe ore was going to the mills! The East needed money! Make way! The mining district, self-organized into Washoe County, had petitioned the California legislature for admittance. Their plea sounded feebly on the Pacific coast, even though the majority of the population was from California. Lincoln, however, had his eye on this little-known area, and Congress began to realize its importance when civil war threatened. Just before Lincoln was inaugurated, it had hurriedly created a Territory of Nevada and Buchanan had signed the bill on March 2, 1861. Then, on July 15, James Nye, appointed by Lincoln, had arrived from New York as the territory's first governor. He was amazed to learn that the camp of Virginia was a six-month-old city with five trustees, a roaring brass band, and high-stepping Union Guards. For one day the miners hid their rowdiness. Two-hundred-and-ten-pound William Stewart saw to that!

"Bullyragging Bill," who had risen from bullwhacker to become the most eminent lawyer on the lode, was staunchly admired by John Mackay. A driving, highhanded man of tremendous energy, and a tough fighter with fists, gun, or words, William M. Stewart ruled the Comstock. Mackay could never hope to be such a master, he told himself. The miners wanted a showman for a leader, one who could dramatize their emotions, make them laugh or cry at will. He wouldn't make even a good politician, for his first thought was to appeal to reason and not feelings. Mackay shied from crowds, stuttered when excited, and was no speechmaker at any time. How then did he stand a chance of becoming a power on the great treasure vein?

Returning to his six-dollar-a-day salary as shift boss for Mexican, he watched many a Secessionist and Unionist wrangle in the subterranean chambers. He saw that new patriotic fuel would have to be added soon if the kettle of conflict were to continue boiling, as trouble at home in the form of disputed mining claims had occupied general attention. Uncertainty of boundary lines had attracted to the lode designing individuals bent on promoting costly litigation, and in September of 1861, the first of 245 suits pertaining to titles began.

A combination of capitalists, who controlled the leading mines, supported William Stewart's opinion that the Comstock Lode was but a single vein. Pitted against them were the small individual owners with parallel locations, who insisted that the great deposit of metal was composed of many ledges. Mackay had tramped over every part of the region and was certain that it consisted of many small, detached ranges of quartz forming a broad, continuous belt—a broken fissure, filled to overflowing with metals gathered and dropped by ancient seas.

3

All enthusiasm for the Civil War departed with the rare clouds of summer. The sun was setting early. Darkness and the coolness of a shaded, disapproving mountainside descended on the Comstock at three in the afternoon. As the snow covered the crimson-tinted hills to the east, men of eighty-six mining companies tramped up and down the steep streets of

Virginia, complaining of the bitter nights and of the slush which had transformed sodden slopes into dangerous slides.

The hundreds of goats that had taken possession of every hill and gully sought shelter in abandoned tunnels such as Mackay's. The "boys" began to haunt the warm, brightly lit barrooms. Jack O'Brien took his chance at twenty-one or faro "out of hand"—dealt by a woman instead of from the box. Men who had never thought of gambling came to join the game in order to gaze at her, for women were scarce and highly respected. Mackay had no interest in faro and did not frequent the dance hall with its four Teutonic girls, or did he listen to the hurdy-gurdy. Only occasionally would he join the restless gambling crowd in the too-bright saloons. He preferred to nourish his inquisitive mind on good authors by the flickering light of a kerosene lamp in his cabin. It was so hard to climb!

"Why should I bother with cards?" he would ask Jack. "I can sit in on a far more exciting game of chance—a pick-and-shovel game that might reveal at any moment a true bonanza."

He was playing against a silent opponent in the heart of an inscrutable mountain. This contest would require a clear head and far more skill than pedro or monte. What did he care for hard liquor, when beneath his feet ran a stream more intoxicating than whiskey, with a glow more lasting than champagne? When he visited the spacious Crystal Bar, it was only for a few minutes. Why loll night after night on its walnut counter and gaze stupidly at its sparkling decanters or at one's own reflection in the massive mirror? Let the others listen to the oaths and boisterous laughter, the constant rattle of dice, the roll of the spinning ball, the ring of coin, the slap of dirty cards on the sticky table tops.

John Mackay, who never laughed loudly and seldom audibly, had to get away from this noise. Out into the darkness he would go. He did not realize that he had a companion on the mountain shelf. Unseen beside him stood another miner, his head uplifted, his sleeves uprolled—a young man of identical age and inheritance, with brown eyes as sparkling as the metalliferous ore beneath his feet, with hair as black as the raven's wing.

There stood two men whose lives had been singularly arranged from birth to run in parallel grooves for thirty-seven years. And when their paths converged on the horizon of the Comstock, the concussion was to rock a great frontier to its foundation. The gods of Ireland had placed in their veins blood as rich as the precious ore of the mountains, a life stream impregnated with the red and white corpuscles of material success—high intelligence, and an ambition that dared to soar beyond the clouds.

4

The birth of James Fair in Clougher, near Belfast, Ireland, had occurred just five days after that of John Mackay; but he was not to arrive in America until the elder lad had been selling papers along Park Row for two years. The Fair brood of six children was accompanied by only the Scotch-Irish father, the mother having refused to come to the New World. This family did not stop in New York City, but hurried on to Geneva, Illinois, where the children began to attend public school. However, James Fair, Sr., had no intention of remaining long in the Prairie State. His gaze was fixed on a farm in Alabama.

Jimmie, fourth son and youngest child, was only twelve and needed a guardian. Thus it was that he was transferred to Chicago and placed in the care of Mr. Mosely, a lawyer friend of the father's. Parents are not so easily replaced in a strange land, and during the next several years, the pseudo-orphan "had many a long night crying." John Mackay had at least a mother's companionship through his teens.

"I never had any pleasure as a boy ... I never was a boy. ... I was always full of care as long as I can remember," Fair frequently said.[1]

Mr. Mosely saw that his young charge was an unusually alert fellow and promptly placed him in an academy. Fair had had no formal education. When not studying, he became very helpful in looking up authorities for his attorney-guardian. It was this skill in quickly locating the exact law reference which convinced Mr. Mosely that this should be the boy's career.

The handsome, curly-headed lad, however, found other studies more to his liking. Born in a family of mechanics, it was but natural that mathematics, chemistry, and all scientific subjects should be his favorites.

He had very positive ideas regarding his future. "The law office is not for me, Mr. Mosely," he said. "I was not born to settle other men's quarrels."[2]

He carefully looked over other professions where a possible fortune could be made.

"I started in on a paper in Chicago," Fair related years later, "and a week was enough for me to see that a man didn't make any money there, so I quit."[3]

After eight years of schooling, James Fair gained in the race with John Mackay. Early in the flush year of the gold rush, he started across the plains for California with a party of emigrants—two wagons and several riding horses.

"I had to take charge of that company, boy as I was, in order to keep those men from killing each other," Fair insisted. "They were men of means and good standing and character ... but they became so peevish from the wear and tear upon the system by the daily marching, that they were just like children. I used to get on my horse and go miles ahead, find a good place to camp, stick a ramrod down to show it was taken, and go back to meet them."

Always the leader, never the follower.

The journey ended in August at Lassen's rancho, and from there Fair came down to Long Bar in the Feather River country for his first mining. He did not intend to dig for long. He had come west to command men by the thousands and control money that flowed in millions. These intentions were not kept secret. To everyone he repeated, "I do not intend to lead a poor mans' life."[4]

Yet success for James Fair was not to be immediate. Long Bar, on *El Río de las Plumas,* was barren ground for treasure hunters. The party went on to Rich Bar on the north fork. Here Fair advised the men to go to work on the bar instead of attempting to divert the water and work the floor of the stream. He began to construct wheelbarrows with rawhide tires for hauling the gravel to the river waters.

This work finished, he determined to reveal still greater genius for invention. It was painfully slow work to wield the heavy rockers by hand, so he built a device that handled thirty times as much dirt as before. Cutting down two trees and hollowing them out canoe-shape, he anchored them in midstream. These supported a great water wheel which furnished the power for running the rockers. Fair next ordered the building of a dam above the diggings which not only laid bare the river bottom but diverted the flow through a series of troughlike logs to the dry hill being worked. Still the work produced no great profit so, in the spring, Fair decided to break camp.

While walking past the sluices one morning he glanced carelessly into one of them, and there he saw a scattered panful of gold lodged in the rough niches. Fair hurried down the hill and cried, "Heavens, boys, we have struck it now!"[5]

From Rich Bar he filled his sacks to overflowing with fine ore, and took it to the new Wells, Fargo bank in Sacramento for deposit.

John Mackay would have to hurry to get ahead of this inventive fellow with his remarkable powers of adaption. Yet Fair had none of the plodding patience of his rival. He was forever off on a new scent.

The Jackson mine at Shaw's Flat, Table Mountain, was his next camp, and then Poorman's Creek, which had just been discovered. The latter was rich in gold, so Fair's fortune increased considerably.

Here in 1851 he met the Jim and Bill of Mackay's later acquaintance in San Francisco. "Flood and O'Brien had a little general merchandise stock—plenty of flour and bacon and such things," Fair recounted in later days. "I could not have told you their last names then to save my life."[6]

At this time, Mackay had just landed in San Francisco and was heading up toward the mountains. Fate, fearful that their paths might cross before she was ready, turned Fair's attention to agriculture. He took out his bank roll of several thousand dollars, purchased a large farm one mile out of Petaluma, and abandoned his mining career. Drought one year and rust the next completely satisfied his agricultural ambitions. His money had gone into the surface soil as easily as Mackay's had rolled down the tunnel. Back to the mines he had to go for more.

Table Mountain attracted him again. Near Caldwell's Gardens, the Whimtown of later years, he continued to develop his natural bent. At the same time, with the aid of two other men, Patton and Caldwell, he purchased a quartz mill at Angels Camp. The pair soon sold out to Irwin Davis, who helped Fair develop the Utica mine and handle the ore of the district.

This was Fair's first quartz mining. Their mill, with its up-to-date machinery, ranked with the foremost mills in California. It was chosen to crush one of the first mule-back shipments of Washoe ore. Even before Mackay reached the Comstock, Fair was convinced that its quartz could be worked readily.

There was one serious drawback, however. The cost of transportation over the mountainous wagon roads was outrageous. If he was to mill ore from Utah Territory, it must be at the actual scene of mining.

May of 1860 saw Fair crossing the great range. "The first visit ... looked like a mere goose chase," Fair confessed, "and I thought to myself that I would not give my mills and mines in Calaveras for any uncertain thing like that. It contained no prominent bodies of ore, except in a very few places. But in a few months I returned, it opened up and looked better."[7]

This time Fair studied carefully the assumed line of the fissure, and "was convinced there was something stable about it." In both Gold Hill and Virginia City he located small claims, then hurried away to Humboldt County. He, too, knew that it would take a gold mine to work the silver vein, so he built a fine mill on the Sheba River at Star City, the profits from which were to be his means of exploring the wonder vein. He secured a capable crew of men to manage the mill, installed the first self-working furnaces ever used, and, when everything was in order, returned to the Comstock.

Mackay and Fair, beginning with the identical narrow ambitions, were both heading relentlessly for the very heart of the Comstock Lode. Mackay of the light drooping mustache and hard-hitting fists was completely happy only when in the company of a few friends. Being distrustful of his conversational powers, he did more thinking than talking. Blackbearded Fair, with a knife in his bootleg, was an extremely sociable fellow, of easy humor and natural bonhomie, an adapt distributor of blarney. With natures as diametrically opposed as this, would these fortune seekers meet as friends or foes?

3   Springboard to Fortune

1

"Labor is enough capital for any healthy young person, and through labor I'll earn my place as manager and master of the greatest mines in the world," asserted John Mackay to his skeptical acquaintances. Then wealth was not his main goal.

This attitude appeared anomalous to the other miners. They didn't argue the point with him, however, for already in 1862 the Comstock was beginning to cast furtive glances at this aggressive fellow who asked odds from no one but who invariably demanded his dues. His natural reticence and shy demeanor fooled many who judged him hastily.

From childhood Mackay had been taught that labor was omnipotent. With the physical and mental equipment bestowed upon him by a hardy race, he was confident that he could reach the top. Mining would be his career since, to him, money procured from the treasures of the earth was the cleanest form of wealth one could seek. His fortune would be made in an honest way, he told himself, and not through stock manipulations that injure many.

But although his grip was on the pick, he understood its limits. His thoughts were far ahead of its stroke. What matter how he moved forward toward his fortune, as long as he kept the same direction. From wealth would come power, and from power the new harmonies of life to satisfy those inner yearnings. Thus Mackay wove the web of his fate.

The first six months of 1862 were not encouraging. The spring floods again caused great disaster in the mines. "The earth softened and ceased to be ... self-supporting. All now rested on a few crazy timbers which speedily gave way, and all Gold Hill tumbled down and shut up," stated the *Territorial Enterprise*. The Piutes insisted that the coming of the whites had changed the climate of the state.

However, in a few weeks the same journal stated that "Most of the quartz mills about Virginia, Gold Hill and Silver City are again repaired and in running order, and would be making money as before, but for the present high prices of fuel and costs of hauling rock, both of which have been nearly doubled since the storms. Another cause which advances the cost of reducing ores is found in the increased price of labor, consequent on the emigration to the northern mines (Humboldt)."

With enough money now to pay for his room and board, Mackay sought lodging at "Noisy" Brown's on B Street. The lode was exceedingly dull. If money was to return to circulation, it must come from California. Quiet hung over the huge quartz vein, "now a bewildering maze of whims and windlasses, ore-bins and sheds, shoots and car-tracks perched high in the air on their supports and intricate trestle-work, smoke stacks, workshops, and dwelling houses."

With the approach of the Fourth of July there was a revival of interest in the Civil War. Mackay and the Unionists had a drink of "Yank's Best" in anticipation of the promised cessation of hostilities. The "fire-eaters" still loyal to the Southern cause, ordered big horns of "Lightning Whiskey." But their hopes soon faded as the war went on.

John Mackay took great interest in one soldier of the Union—"Unconditional Surrender Grant," the newspapers called him. Who was this unprecedented fighter who used a bulldog strategy unknown to warring nations, who won battles as casually as he trimmed his beard, and who captured an entire army in the course of an afternoon? He was a future President of the United States whose path was not likely to cross that of a Nevada miner.

By July 14, the Civil War was again in the background. The troops sent to the lode when sentiment threatened to run high, were no longer needed.

"We never talk in Washoe about anything except dips, curves, angles, veins, lodes, spurs, and collateral leads," the *Enterprise* corrected the impression of the West. "Occasionally a Secesh and a Union man, owning in the same lead, limber up and throw a big battle in each other's face, but merely to vary the monotony of the conversation."

The fact that the War of Secession did not end on the

Fourth was the turning point in John Mackay's career. Its continuation for three more years provided him with the great opportunity of his life.

2

Mackay learned that the owners of the Kentuck mine in Gold Hill were trying to incorporate its 94 feet into shares, following the example set by Ophir. Up to this time the actual measurement of the claims determined the number of "feet" or shares held by the owners. San Francisco had recently organized a stock exchange, and Kentuck, eager to be out in front, decided to increase its shares by forming a company. One serious factor made this impossible. A shareholder was missing. Being a loyal Southerner, this individual had left some months before to join the army of the Confederacy. Whether he was dead or still alive, no one could hazard a guess.

Meanwhile Mackay had thoroughly inspected the Kentuck mine. He was certain it was rich in bullion. James Clair Flood and William Shoney O'Brien knew this too. As early as 1862 they had begun to operate in this mine, along with the Crown Point and Belcher mines. The two men had opened up the Auction Lunch saloon on Washington Street, between Montgomery and Sansome, in San Francisco, and were catering to a fine clientele. Having thus daily contact with prominent mining men and stockbrokers, Flood and O'Brien appeared to be stepping into the financial circles of the city. Mackay had been keeping his eye on them. If his break came, he would need associates. Organization alone would be able to beat the Comstock.

When a liberal bonus was offered to the person who could obtain the deed to Kentuck's missing "feet," Mackay's mind worked like a reflex. He must take advantage of this turn in events. His first grubstake had been made in Kentucky—perhaps it was a lucky word for him. He'd go back and climb, if necessary, Pinnacle Mountain to locate the Southerner who preferred to fight for a cause rather than struggle for a fortune on an indifferent frontier where loyalties shifted with the Washoe hurricanes.

Mackay's work as an ordinary miner apparently had not made him shortsighted, for, without a word to anyone, he disappeared. A Unionist was going into the camp of the enemy to chase a will-o'-the-wisp, to run not only the risk of

being unable to penetrate the army lines but of failing to pro-
cure the valuable slip of paper once he found his man.

One disheartening month followed another as he tried to
learn the whereabouts of the Kentuck shareholder. The war-
torn South did not know where anyone was today or where
he would be tomorrow. For nearly ten months John Mackay
followed the elusive trail. When he returned to Virginia City
in 1863 he appeared to take but little less risk than he had in
the South, since the Washoe zephyr that heralded his arrival
might well have been shot from a smoking howitzer.

Mackay's acquaintances sought him out now, amazed at
the unexpectedness of his plunge in Kentuck. They were eager to learn if it contained a bonanza.

"I really wouldn't care to say," he told them. "You know,
'salting' of mines has returned with three-card monte and
'prick the loop.' "

Exasperating fellow! Too closemouthed!

The first specimens of ore removed from the mine were
very promising. Blue- and white-streaked quartz, speckled
with pinheads of gold and silver, caused the men to work
with full speed. A tunnel fifty feet long had already been dug
along the blind ledge. At two hundred feet the pay dirt would
be hit, the owners were promised.

During Mackay's absence a new game had been invented,
the game of "freeze-out." The monied interests would get
control of the stock by first working to lower the price. They
did this by offering their own shares at a reduced figure, then
had agents buy in privately all the stock of the other shareholders who were induced to sell at the low figure. The moment the mine was in their control, they started to misman-
age it, deliberately levying heavy assessments to force out any
remaining small shareholder.

When Mackay discovered that he too was in line to feel
the claws of the "bears," he determined not to relinquish his
stocks at any cost. Once again he looked about him for a
partner in Kentuck, as this mine was to be the pivot of his
future activities on the lode.

James M. Walker, brother of the future governor of the
state of Virginia, asked Mackay to join him, and the two
men owned a substantial block of stock when the title to the
Kentuck mine was perfected in 1865.

3

With added prestige from his clever stroke of buying into the Kentuck mine, John Mackay was made superintendent of the Caledonia Tunnel and Mining Company. Up to the time that he took charge, this Gold Hill mine had paid no dividends, so he was bent on hitting its streak of fat, if such existed.

The workmen soon grew to like their new boss. He let them call him John, and, as one miner expressed it, "We feel as if we're working with him instead of for him." In spite of his abrupt manner and occasional drastic procedure, Mackay had a way with these men. His pulse had beat in unison with theirs too long for him not to understand the miner's temperament. His brusqueness and unsocial tendency did not make him unjust in his decisions. The workmen knew that he never lied to them, and although he remained remote, they could approach him unhesitatingly with their problems. Mackay never failed to listen courteously, and then take prompt action on any matter. Little by little he drew out the best there was in his men.

Discouragement came from another source—the mine itself. American Flat, which housed the Caledonia, was troubled with creeping clay. A two-inch streak of slowly moving soil would begin to rise on the floor of the tunnel; in a few days it had grown into a band thirty inches across. Almost imperceptible in motion, there was no limit to its power. The surrounding rock, forced to give way under this irresistible pressure, crushed timbers and closed up drifts at will. New streaks appeared from time to time to carry on the destruction.

The inchoate empire of Mount Davidson had accepted the masterful rule of the heavily whiskered Stewart because he confined his activities to its surface. But these meddling sappers who were digging a city beneath its crust would not find victory such a simple matter. At the moment only five mines were removing pay dirt—Gould & Curry, Savage, Ophir, Mexican, and Potosi. Still the Comstock refused to hang its head. Whole ranges of frame and brick buildings continued to spring up along A, B, and C Streets. Lots jumped in price from a few hundred dollars to thousands.

"Many of the houses would look fine even on Montgomery Street," boasted the *Enterprise* to San Francisco. "We have stores just as large and almost as well stocked as stores on Front or J Streets, Sacramento; and three churches. . . ."

Virginia was beginning at last to recognize the Sabbath. Mackay, too, attended the Catholic church more regularly.

"There are plenty of raisins in this huge plum pudding," he kept asserting as his fingers stretched out for twenty-five thousand of them. That, in dollars, was Mackay's idea of a fortune. In a short time his dream became a reality as Kentuck's shares began to soar—$1,000, $7,000, $11,000—and double, $22,000 each! One share alone had made him as rich as he had ever thought of being. This was the circumstance that he had made, that was destined to make him. His vivid imagination conjured up a breathing simulacrum of his future person—a Power! Was it vanity that made him want to be superior? Or was it a subconscious feeling of inferiority, due to early poverty and lack of education, that had developed these habits of initiative, this boldness and craving to be spectacular, to show everyone how worth-while he could be—all as compensation for that natural shyness? If acclaim came to John Mackay, then it would be proven whether egotism or this inner limitation was the basic cause for his striving for power.

Unbelievable wealth was his, and with it the framework of his life began to change. The early spark of ambition was fanned into a hot flame. How could he play first fiddle in this Comstock orchestra with its numerous instruments? As superintendent of the Caledonia he was gaining no prestige but at least he was learning his trade.

A fortune in stocks could be lost in a day. He must not go gimcrack like Sandy Bowers in this new role of wealthy man. If he sold his stocks at this time he could build a thirty-thousand-dollar house like Bill Stewart's on Taylor Street. He was able to support a wife now. Perhaps, among the newcomers, there would be a charming girl like Mrs. Stewart, a brunette preferably, with flashing blue eyes.

James Fair had married Theresa Rooney, a young woman educated at Mount St. Vincent in New York. The wedding of Episcopalian and Catholic took place at Angels Camp on the last day of 1861. Two years later, the Fairs came to settle permanently in Virginia.

"I did not want to remain around a dying man," Fair said succinctly, explaining his abandonment of the Humboldt region, "lest I should be taken for the doctor." He imagined that he could conquer the Comstock Lode.

John Mackay knew that to build a mill would be profitable because, as superintendent of a mine, he could contract for the crushing of its ore in his own mill. In addition, a shortage of mills existed. James M. Walker joined him in the erection of the Petaluma mill in 1863. Mackay would not work alone on the Comstock. Though the name, Petaluma, had been a jinx for James Fair, Mackay's move proved to be a good investment.

4

With the first chill winds of October, 1863, sickness and a slackening in trade prevailed. The streets, formerly crowded with vehicles of every description, from twelve-mule, double-decker prairie schooner to Chinaman's woodcart, were deserted. One by one, the close-cramped lodginghouses of summer were vacated; the population dropped from seven thousand to four thousand. This shrinkage was well timed.

At the end of the month half the frame buildings of the greater part of Virginia went up in smoke. The two rival hand fire engines, manned by divekeepers, toughs, and gamblers of every sort, and captained by the most desperate characters of the lot, raced up narrow Taylor Street for the honor of arriving first at the scene of the fire. When one gained the other and attempted to pass, their wheels locked with disastrous results. A battle of knives and pistols then took place while the crackling fire raged unchecked a few blocks away. Fortunately, the wind changed in time to save the mines. With no water pressure, the presence of the fire engines at the scene of disaster would have been only for dramatic effect anyway.

By Christmas the ravages of that conflagration were scarcely noticeable. Southerners had forgotten to attend meetings in Virginia House—the leading hotel on the southeast corner of B and Sutton—in their rush to erect new structures on the ashes of the old. Unionists were likewise occupied, and paid no attention to the rumor that Lincoln wanted to be godfather of a new state and had his eyes focussed on Nevada Territory.

Though the population increased and diminished with the seasons, the number of donkeys in the mining camp continued to mount. One evening, legend tells us, Mackay was walking down the board sidewalks of C Street, the Broadway of Virginia (it having replaced B as the center of activity), on his way to Maguire's Opera House. He carefully picked his way among the protruding spikes shining in the light of the new gas street lamps, and, in doing so, came close to a German miner who was attempting to sell some of the animals to a friend.

"They are wonderful German singers," he was saying to the prospective donkey buyer as Mackay passed.

Catching sight of the mine superintendent, he turned quickly to address him. "How about you, Mr. Mackay? Could you use a few Washoe canaries?"

Mackay answered with his slow smile and Irish accent, "Sorry, fellow. Not interested. But come around when you have a few that sing in Irish."

5

The sinking sun of 1863 cast a frosty redness across the Comstock. Snow and sleet and flannel-swathed necks forced Mackay to abandon the expression, "It's blowing stones today."

During the year seven million dollars' worth of bullion had been removed from the subterranean storehouse, indicating that the infant feet of the lode would soon be stepping into the shoes of the Cyclops. The South and East continued to pay court to the God of War, who had dethroned King Cotton and His Majesty Manufacturing. Though San Francisco was stock-mad, Commerce and the Handicrafts were still its Regents. The Comstock likewise acknowledged fealty to two old monarchs—"feet" and William Stewart. John Mackay, who would win a crown as a master miner, saw his hopes vanish as 1864 inaugurated a four-year period of depression.

Ever since 1860, Washoe had appeared prosperous. Trade had flourished, rents and real estate prices had increased, and credit had been extended to everyone. But Virginia, third city in size and importance in the West, had become a spendthrift on a promise. Its extravagance and display of luxury had soon written up a many-ciphered score against the future, the expenditure of public funds being as unwarranted and reckless as that of private fortunes. With the majority of mines unable to pay even their running expenses, assessments became larger and more frequent, which resulted in many stockholders relinquishing their interests. Thus, from lack of sinking funds, prospecting was stopped on dozens of claims and great unemployment followed. Early in 1863 business began to languish, and by 1864 general inertia and widespread uncertainty prevailed.

In spite of the overused expression, "That's hard papers," and the daily symphony of melancholy, "Borrasca," John Mackay did not curb his activities. The clouds surrounding greater undertakings gradually scattered as Kentuck stock continued to pay rich dividends. James Walker had been a disappointing partner, because he was too cautious; but if Mackay could find other associates who had shrewdness and the gambling heart of Jack O'Brien rolled into one then he would be capable of controlling the forces of this mountain kingdom.

The firm of Flood and O'Brien, partners then for eight years, was cutting a wide swath in San Francisco's financial district by clever manipulations of stocks and properties. A corporation with them would be calculated to effect momentous things. The next time Mackay went to San Francisco he visited the proprietors of the Auction Lunch Saloon, and discussed a partnership with him.

"We'll make plenty of money if we join forces," James Flood assured him.

"It's agreed," responded Mackay, while to himself he whispered, "I intend to be more than a mere money seeker."

Both Flood and O'Brien had had mining experience, but they knew nothing of deep mining. Hence they realized that their activities in Nevada required a minuteman at the very crux of their mining operations. What Mackay claimed to know, he knew accurately. Besides, his spongelike capacity for absorbing and storing away every bit of information dropped would be invaluable to the new company. As a superintendent, Mackay had access to the fifty-seven and one-half miles of estimated workings on the lode, and his studies had not been confined solely to the great fissure. With the eyes of an Argus, he had been watching the men whose names were household words in Washoe. Not their actions but their intentions were his concern. There were so many others who possessed qualities which made them serious rivals.

6

Following the nine-and-a-half-months' siege of Petersburg by that amazing man of perseverance, General Grant, the sunset of the Confederacy provided Washoe with an excuse for celebrating. When the telegraph wires hummed Grant's simple, kindly speech to Lee, "Allow them to take their horses to their homes. They will need them in the spring plowing," the half of Virginia under the brown crust of earth came forth, flag in hand, its best dress on. The daylight portion called out its fire engines, decorated them with bunting, and put them behind its brass bands to parade through the streets. Every mine and every place of business was deserted. Undismayed by the heat, the musicians played everything they knew, from "God Save the Queen" to *Tannhauser*.

Two hundred small Washoeites waved tenpenny flags and piped, "Lincoln!" Indian women with quill-pierced ears paused in their laundering with washing machine and patent wringer to give a guttural grunt. It was a holiday for even the journalists. Only the bartenders were at work, frantically trying to keep pace with the demands of throats hoarse from shouting.

This hilarious jamboree was stilled by the deafening thunderclap of a national catastrophe. Lincoln had been assassinated! Godfather Abe, who had persuaded them, the citizens of Nevada, to come into the Union as the thirty-sixth state on October 31, 1864, the Great Emancipator for whom Washoe had poured out its wealth in order to maintain sufficient credit to carry the Union through to victory, had been taken from them. Secessionists and Unionists sobered up to mourn with the same fervor that had marked their celebration of peace. These miners were not so coarse but that they felt the height of sorrow as well as of joy.

John Mackay, with less outward display of emotion, noticed that the lode was without a tycoon for its booted army. William Stewart had gone to Washington to sit in a senator's chair and promote mining legislation for Washoe. Other ambitious men were running abreast toward the vacated throne—William Sharon of the Bank of California, focussing his lens on the whole of the Comstock; Adolph Sutro of the Tunnel Company, backed by William Stewart as its president; and James Fair, superintendent of the Central mine and the great Ophir Company.

However, a very different fellow from any of these now began to rule John Mackay's life—the unexpected Knave of Hearts.

4 Letting Out the Tucks

1

Laboring in the depths of the mines, John Mackay was not aware that Marie-Louise Bryant, daughter of Colonel Dan Hungerford, had moved to Virginia City following a separation from her husband. After the Piute uprising of 1860, Dr. Edmund Bryant had remained in Nevada to conduct a health resort at Steamboat Springs, thirteen miles northwest of Virginia City. There his wife brought their two children, Eva and Marie, and attempted to make a happy home for the family, but it wasn't long before Dr. Bryant returned to California. It was claimed that he had become addicted to the use of alcohol and drugs. Marie-Louise was left penniless, so she moved to the lode to seek work. Not long afterward, the younger daughter, Marie, passed away, adding further heartbreak to Mrs. Bryant's life.

It was at this time that Father Patrick Manogue of the Catholic church, St. Mary's in the Mountains, discussed her plight with Mackay. Mrs. Moch, a boarding-house keeper, had helped her considerably, he said, but something more had to be done. The kindly priest, a former miner who had worked with Mackay near the forks of the Yuba River, was certain his old acquaintance would head a subscription fund for the young widow. Having met her previously at James Fair's house, Mackay was very happy to raise the sum needed, and in a few days his own contribution was augmented by many hundreds of dollars from others.

One evening after work he brought her the generous gift. High-strung Mrs. Bryant was deeply touched by this gesture from the rough camp, and considerably impressed by the gentle-voiced man who had taken the time to bring it to her.

29

John Mackay was as distinguished in appearance as any man she had met. Standing five feet ten and weighing 165 pounds, the miner walked with the alert, energetic carriage of a person who loves life. Marie-Louise Bryant noticed, also, that when he smiled his deep-set eyes were very warm and friendly.

Before long, Mackay was a frequent visitor to the plank shack on the outskirts of town where the young mother did sewing and taught French for her living. Renting houses was one of the miner's side lines, so he promptly located a more comfortable dwelling for her, and provided her with a few select boarders. This work, however, proved to be of extremely short duration.

Falling in love with dark-haired and blue-eyed Mrs. Bryant was not difficult for the quiet miner. From her French mother, Marie-Louise had inherited a natural social poise, while from Colonel Dan had come the qualities that had made him a fighter—tenacity and ambition. In addition, Mrs. Bryant was well educated, and had devoted a great deal of time to the study of French and music. Mackay's shyness appealed to the strong-minded girl, and his persistent campaign of entertainment was calculated to win the pleasure-starved seamstress.

In the spring when the sunflowers covered the hillsides in profusion, John Mackay would seat her behind a span of spirited horses and drive her over the new Geiger Grade to Carson City, or down the canyon to see the few apple, pear, and cherry trees recently planted, the one vegetable garden that defied the desert, and the three new sluices installed for saving the silver sulphurets from the tailings.

On hot summer Sundays they went picnicking among the sagebushes under the shade of an umbrella. There were also occasional swims at the Gould & Curry reservoir, a pool lined with shanty dressing rooms and a saloon.

When the Fourth of July brought all the Piutes to town, and the lode put on its gayest dress, Mackay and Mrs. Bryant joined the crowds at the new soda fountain, the first one installed in Nevada, and paid one long bit (fifteen cents) per glass for refreshments.

With the provokingly bad weather of fall, they moved indoors for the numerous socials in the Athletic Hall, the church festivals, the concerts, benefits, and balls. How Mrs. Bryant liked to dance! Everyone danced in the Sagebrush State, everyone except ministers of the gospel and octogenarians. Shuffling, bowing, scraping, crossing over in the changing of partners, to the music of the chassé or the waltz, Marie-Louise Bryant never grew tired.

In the winter Mackay escorted her to Piper's Opera House, opposite Dan Lyon's saloon on D Street. No one could have made an entrance more skillfully. Miss Amy Stone, playing in "Fanchon, the Cricket," didn't get all of the audience's attention the night that Mrs. Bryant occupied John Mackay's new box, her finely striped dress set off by a small square of velvet tied flat on the top of her head. Her dark hair was done up in the height of fashion—with "rats" and "mice." Dress-circle and orchestra seats were one dollar, parquet, fifty cents, but the seamstress sat in a five-dollar private box.

For the miners the Washoe month had only half as many days as in other places, ending abruptly on the fifteenth when all coin was spent. To the wealthy mineowner, waiting for his marriage (the event had been set for November 25, 1867), it had twice as many days as it should have had. Louisa, as she was called, was twenty-four years of age on her wedding day; Mackay was but three days under thirty-six. There was no hilariousness, no charivariing after the ceremony in Jim Fair's home, because Virginia City knew that cowbell and kettle serenades did not fit quiet John Mackay.

The couple moved into a very plain home, even though Kentuck was paying a three-hundred-dollar dividend on each share. The young wife thought frequently of Bob Graves's Castle with its three stories of white woodwork and plum-colored wallpaper, its Bohemian mirrors and Italian fireplaces, its gorgeous crystal chandelier brought from France—of the butler and footman waiting in alcoves near the entrances for the sound of the heavy knocker. That's what she could have right now if her husband weren't so unpretentious. That's what she meant to have, but not in this mining camp. Nob Hill in San Francisco, with its wealthy Crockers, Huntingtons, and Stanfords, was to be her future home. From that sacred hill of social eminence, of secret duels and open court fights, beautiful Mrs. Mackay intended to soar.

"She did not need to adapt herself to the new position and the dazzling sphere created for her by her husband's wealth. She was gifted with that rare nature and character which fit one to use the best as well as the ordinary gifts of fortune."[1]

Mrs. Mackay was already dreaming of being the leader of America's social world. How would she be able to accomplish this, married to a person whose brusqueness around men, and extreme confidence when battling nature, were only a protective coloring for a temperament that actually shrank from wide social contacts and publicity of any kind? Though John took keen interest in discussions of art and literature, as well as the daily topics of conversation, he expressed his opinions only to a few choice friends.

2

"Virginia is now like a big cheese, pretty well gutted, with not much left but the rind. There being nothing else left, the lawyers have started in after the rind." Thus the *Territorial Enterprise* summarized the situation at Christmas of 1867.

Still, John Mackay, like the blooded dogs used that December for badger baiting, was following a promising trail. A fresh coalition had been formed, one that would influence his public life as much as his marriage would effect his private existence. James Fair from Angels Camp had joined the Mackay, Walker, Flood, and O'Brien team. Mackay believed that Fair knew something of geology; Fair was convinced that Mackay was honest and had considerable money.

The two men met one day at the mines and began a lively discussion of Ireland, early life in America, and, finally, their parents. Fair tried to remember if his father had been naturalized. Mackay remarked that his parent had taken out the first citizenship papers, but he was vague regarding the second. To make certain they were American citizens, the pair decided to be naturalized. In short order they were declared bona fide citizens with all attendant privileges, but only Mackay's name appeared on the list of registered voters in the city of Virginia, published April 24, 1867. Fair took little interest in voting, and during his lifetime cast his ballot only twice for president of the United States. Yet there was something intangible in that short civil ceremony that drew the two miners a little closer together, and made them tolerate, in succeeding years, a familiarity from each other that would not, ordinarily, have been permitted.

For a brief period Mackay was superintendent of the Milton mine, but it conflicted with the Chollar so was absorbed by it. Then Mackay became trustee as well as superintendent of the Bullion Mining Company, having purchased 105 of its worthless shares. This mine, located on the Divide between Gold Hill and Virginia, never produced a cent over expenses, but it further developed Mackay's bent for leadership. His reputation for good judgment and uprightness began to spread throughout the mines.

Fair, like Mackay, was born to command and not to obey. At this time he was superintendent of the Hale & Norcross, Gould & Curry, Ophir, and Central mines. As the latest addition to the round table of experts, he was a painstaking worker. Mackay agreed with the *San Francisco Alta* that "It is a matter of satisfaction to get hold of the annual report of the Gould & Curry Company. The sums are almost like those in the financial account of a kingdom, and there is a fullness, explicitness, and frankness of statement which is very valuable to silver mines, and which is not practised eleswhere."[2]

The two San Francisco members of this new combination, Flood and O'Brien, like the Mackay-Fair team, were of identical age, both having been born in 1826.

William Shoney O'Brien came to New York from Stradbally, near Dublin, Ireland. In 1847 he obtained his citizenship and two years later followed other adventurous Americans around Cape Horn. Shortly after his arrival in San Francisco on the *Tarolinta*, O'Brien became associated with Colonel William C. Hoff. The partnership lasted until 1851, when W. J. Romer induced him to share his ship chandlery enterprises. This led to his fortunate connection with James Flood in May of 1854.

Jolly, upright, and respected, Billy O'Brien had no other interests as a member of the Mackay firm than to increase his knowledge of mining stocks and to cement a friendship with Flood that was destined to endure for a quarter of a century. The relationship between the two was ideal from the beginning, since bachelor O'Brien was always a follower. When defeated for election to the California legislature in 1862, he had been highly elated.

James Clair Flood had had a career similar to that of O'Brien. Born on Long Island, of parents in ordinary circumstances, he had received a practical education in the common schools of New York. When the family moved to Fort Hamilton, New York, the bright, industrious boy took up the wheelwright business of his father. This did not suit his ambitious nature, so he too followed the gold trail in 1849. His ship, the *Elizabeth Ellen,* anchored in San Francisco Bay on September 18, after a slow trip around the Horn.

With only good health, a stout frame, and a sanguine temperament to support his slender funds, he departed immediately for the Yuba River to earn his living with a rocker. In two years he saved three thousand dollars, enough, he figured, for the establishment of a small business.

He went to New York City to invest his money but, fortunately for him, could find no suitable undertaking for such a small sum.

Returning to San Francisco, he engaged in various pursuits for the next few years, most of them profitable. A restaurant on Washington Street, near Sansome, was instrumental in making a success of the retail liquor business he established with O'Brien.

Mackay, Fair, Flood, O'Brien and Walker were the important members of the new mining firm. With investments in the Savage, Best & Belcher, Gould & Curry, Utah, Mexican, and Sierra Nevada mines, the group was firmly entrenched on the Comstock.

3

Mrs. Mackay was laying her plans for the future and had her husband legally adopt little Eva Bryant. Just as marriage had taken off the rough edges of his nature, so was Virginia beginning to lose its raw demeanor.

Animate C Street, the New Montgomery of the silver city, was lined with unexcelled restaurants, large shops, glittering saloons, and the new International Hotel. The poorest and yet the best-dressed man on the lode was once again the gambler who found it easy to make a "scratch" at faro or borrow breakfast money. Most of the mines had been reincorporated into shares on the San Francisco stock exchange. Everyone continued to dabble in stocks, from the melancholy darky who blacked one's boots with the dirge of Imperial's latest collapse to the chatty hotel clerk whose Yellow Jacket had just struck a good vein on the 900-foot level. Money was spent rashly on roses, geraniums, freesias, verbenas, and oleanders.

The refining influence of the stage became apparent in June of 1867 when John McCullough came to Virginia City for a series of Shakespearean dramas. His performances resulted in the purchase of thirty costly editions of Shakespeare's complete works, Mackay being one of the buyers.

It was but fourteen hours by the Donner Lake route to connections with the San Francisco cars. The name of John Mackay began to appear more frequently than before on the lists of the Wells, Fargo stages, since he had much to plan with Flood and O'Brien. A conflict was coming up with the new monopoly of the West, the Bank of California, headed by William Ralston and William Sharon. The apple of discord was to be the Hale & Norcross mine.

4

Before one can appreciate the task lying before the Mackay firm one must examine the new palatine of the Comstock, an unknown, who replaced the powerful Stewart. At the very time that the Pacific coast was being shaken from neck to heel by the shocking darma of the Civil War, a little fellow, weighing less than 130 pounds, with the dainty hands of a lady, had taken the whip dropped by William Stewart, to rule the lode more surely than the lawyer had ever dreamed of doing. Here was one of the champion gamecocks against whom Mackay had pitted himself. At the moment, Mackay was spurred with James Fair, but how long easy-talking Fair would be on his side was enigmatical.

There was little of the leader in Sharon's appearance. Forty-two years of age, with dull sandy hair above a high forehead, large nose beneath cold grey eyes, carefully trimmed beard repeating the color of the long mustache, he did not appear to be a man who would appeal to the Comstock. Only two characteristics marked him as a potential leader—the jutting underlip and the poise of the head.

How had this person, so clean as to appear weak, so reserved as to appear unfriendly, replaced a domineering leader? With what impressive strategy had he initiated a new period on this frontier, a decade of authority under a single organization, when individual interests were only pawns?

Fourteen years of real-estate dealings in San Francisco had netted Sharon $150,000. Meanwhile, the city had become a huge gambling den. Sharon took a plunge in mining stocks, hoping to double his fortune, but the unexpected slump of 1864 on the lode caused securities to drop overnight, and he became penniless in a short time. In the midst of the Comstock depression, the directors of the Bank of California decided to establish a branch at Virginia City. W. C. Ralston, the manager, appointed William Sharon as their agent, since he had previously handled to their satisfaction another deal there. Sharon's gambling spirit seemed to Ralston a necessary factor for the daring plan he had in mind. The two men were of the same kidney.

At this time the local banking houses were loaning money to mill and mineowners at the exorbitant rate of 3 per cent to 5 per cent a month. Sharon promptly announced that his firm would charge but 1 per cent. Since capital was extremely timid, due to the constant threat of litigation, owners of Comstock mining property came forward eagerly for large advances.

In a short time one mill after another became idle due to the lack of ore extraction. With stockholders refusing to pay further assessments, the mines could supply only a few mills, and a silent mill was a great expense on account of taxes, insurance, and repairs. Thus Sharon obtained the Swansea mill on an overdue note, and by the spring of 1867 he had added six others to the bank's list. To manage them, and to purchase more mills, he organized the Union Mill and Mining Company with an imposing directorate—William Ralston, D. O. Mills, Alvinza Hayward, William E. Barron, Thomas Sunderland, Charles Bonner, and himself.

Mackay was quick to realize that this company would be an active, controlling agent on the lode in a few months, and have a serious grip on the state's growing industry. With the close of 1867, market rates took a rise of from $15 to $975 a foot, an aggregate increase of $3,000,000. Though 33 per cent to 40 per cent of the ore mined was still being thrown away for lack of facilities to handle it, and even though few mines had been paying, San Francisco contained a sufficient number of gamblers willing to be "washoed" to keep interest alive. Thus, with the advent of a new king on the Comstock, an organized Mackay camp to dethrone him, earthquakes, smallpox, and the first double-bock beer this side of the mountains, good times returned with 1868, the most promising year since 1863.

5

James Fair would have us believe that for a couple of years he had been one of the leading stockholders in the Hale & Norcross mine, along with Charles Low and Irwin Davis, but late in 1867 it was revealed that the Bank of California hirelings had bought heavily of its shares.

Fair, as its assistant superintendent, had indicated to his confederates that this mine had rich unexplored territory. He was reinvesting in it. John Mackay inspected the ground and was also convinced that here was promised a bonanza. From a fifteen-cent low, the individual shares rose to $1,260 in January of 1868, and to $7,100 a month later. Mackay could not buy at this price. Even when the shares dropped to $2,-900 a few days before the March election of trustees, there were none for sale.

The bank had become suspicious the moment the shares rocketed. To prevent anyone else from gaining control at the coming election, the bank forged five shares owned by a woman who was traveling in Germany at the time. The consternation of the new pretenders to the throne was great when, on March 10, they were defeated by two and one-half votes instead of winning by what they had considered a safe margin.

It was several weeks before the owner of the forged stock returned and exposed the fraud. By the time a decision was won in court by the irate shareholder, the prize had been neatly tucked away for the year.

William Sharon laughed softly into his neatly trimmed goatee as Norcross stocks dropped to $41.50 within the next six months. He would teach these small fry a lesson for meddling with the greatest financial organization in the West. Little did he realize that he was dealing with men of infinite resource and perseverance who had met discouragement and defeat before. He would have to do more than just keep his eyes on them.

"In order to keep Sharon's eyes off me," Fair said, "I went over to Field's District, Idaho, and there I put up a 40-stamp mill on the Rising Star mine. In fact I wanted him to think I was broke and had to follow my trade ... and every indication that I could make was to carry that idea out. I really wanted to throw him off his guard."[3]

Fair always claimed that he never invested in the Rising Star mine itself, but merely reaped a handsome profit from the mill. However, since Mackay lost some three hundred thousand dollars during that one year in Idaho, it is likely that his partner lost considerable, too.

Fair returned to the lode the latter part of 1868, and entered into a verbal agreement with Mackay, Flood and O'Brien to make a combined effort to gain control of the Hale & Norcross mine at the 1869 election. Mackay was to take a three-eighths interest, Flood and O'Brien the same amount, and Fair two-eighths.

To the mining men of the lode this struggle for the Norcross was nothing short of ridiculous. The mine had never paid a dividend, and at the close of the fiscal year of 1868 had yielded only 16,536 tons of exceedingly low-grade ore.

However, the next election was weighty with consequences. John Mackay began to worry. Where could he borrow the sixty thousand dollars he needed to invest in Hale & Norcross stock? Even if he could scrape up this amount, there were overwhelming possiblities of ore exhaustion. Of the eleven bonanzas discovered up to this time, practically all had been picked clean.

6

An incident occurred that excluded any thought of surrender on Mackay's part. He met William Sharon in the Bank of California just before closing time one day. Their conversation began calmly enough, but in a short time their bristling voices attracted general attention. The tangle continued somewhat in this fashion:

"Hold on there, Mackay, you're nothing but an ordinary miner, and mark my words, you'll pack your blankets out of this town and over the grade the same way you came in." This bold assertion came from a frail little fellow with an anemic appearance.

William Sharon was addressing an erect, well-knit man whose ruddy face was very red with anger. At this moment Mackay stepped back a pace to permit a well-directed punch across the intervening rail. His voice choked with fury as he attempted to answer.

Controlling himself in a moment, he managed huskily, "You will? Very well, I will still h-have a m-m-mighty sight the b-best of you: I c-can do it!"[4]

With that Mackay strode out of the building.

A few months later, on a miserable day in January, Mackay was walking along B Street, his customary oiled step lagging as his glance followed the gigantic columns of snow that eddied about Mount Davidson. Like disembodied ghosts of "washoed" speculators, these misty clouds appeared to be wandering about, viewing once more the scene of their misfortune, just as Mackay was reflecting upon his unwise investment in Idaho.

"What's the matter there, Mr. Mackay?" a voice interrupted his thoughts. "You look disgusted."

Mackay looked up at Billy Wood, attorney for the bank crowd and future representative of Mackay himself.

"Well, things aren't so g-good, I'll c-c-confess. I need sixty thousand d-dollars."

"How soon do you have to have it?" questioned the lawyer.

"Today. Otherwise I'll l-lose stocks that I'm sure I c-c-can increase at least twenty times by March."[5]

"Hmmm. Well, maybe we can do something about it," Wood assured him. "Have you the time to step up to my office now? Sunderland should be there."

Mackay accompanied him to the Bank of California and repeated his story to Mr. Wood's associate. Sunderland requested a list of the stock he was trying to hold, then disappeared downstairs. Within ten minutes he was back.

"Here's your money, Mr. Mackay," he addressed the astonished borrower as he handed over a check and a note to be signed. "It will be satisfactory with us if you bring in your stocks later."

Mackay signed the slip of paper and returned it to Sunderland before glancing at the check. When he saw who made out a personal check to him, he was amazed.

"Did Sharon d-d-do this?" he asked.[6]

"Yes, he was glad to do you the favor," replied Sunderland. "And let me give you a little advice—you and Sharon are both too hot-tempered to quarrel with each other. When you both feel like fighting at the same time, separate and fight outsiders."[7]

The pair of rivals were, beyond question, hotheaded, but never impetuous. Sharon, however, thought too much of victory and too little of his adversary. Mackay took the sixty thousand dollars and added it to the battle fund of the Hale & Norcross.

Shortly before the March, 1869, election of trustees, William Sharon was bewildered by an item in the *Gold Hill News*. "As James Fair and John W. Mackay, of Virginia City, own over four hundred shares of Hale & Norcross stock, they will be likely to control the election of officers in March."

The publication did not know that these two investors were broke at the moment of victory. Mackay had invested $120,-000—half of it Sharon's money; Fair had bought $40,000 worth of stocks—all he could afford as he had invested heavily in San Francisco real estate during the year; Flood and

O'Brien, according to James Walsh, had been forced to borrow $50,000 to carry their share.

James Flood assumed the presidency of the new board of directors, the other members of the firm being trustees. The two San Francisco partners relaxed in the Auction Lunch saloon, "resort for the upper ten," as Fair called it. Fair became superintendent of the Norcross, Mackay being named assistant.

Sharon made a final attempt to direct the handling of the mine. He sought out Mackay to make a bold assertion:

"I know all you care about is winning the fight. Since you have no facilities for handling the ore from a big mine like the Norcross, we will keep right on working it for you."

"The hell you will!" Mackay is said to have shouted at him. "See here, B-Billy Sharon, I'll not only m-m-manage that m-mine myself, but I'll b-b-build all the m-mills I need to work its ore!"

It was Sharon's turn to leave in a dudgeon. He had counted upon at least crushing the Norcross ore since he controlled practically all the mills on the lode.

Mackay was far ahead of the banker. Ten days before the election, he and Fair had climbed into the latter's carriage and driven to Silver City, about five miles below Virginia, where they had purchased the Bacon mill. Mackay didn't tell all he knew, even in anger.

7

During the next three years Sharon, the Bank of California, and the entire mining community watched wide-eyed the progress of the Hale & Norcross under its new management. The very first month the $5.00 assessment was rescinded and shortly an additional $5.00 dividend was declared. In July, 1869, the dividend increased to $6.00, totaling $48,000 for the shareholders.

While Fair was occupied with a lawsuit instigated by H. C. Howard, Mackay purchased for the firm the Trench mill in Silver City and the old Sullivan mill, on the site of which a mill of latest design was to be built. There was baggage of the past to dispose of too—105 shares of Bullion stock which Mackay had bought so confidently as trustee and superintendent of that company. Kentuck asked a ten-dollar assessment in July, due to the closing of its shaft following the horrible conflagration of April 8. With the Bullion Mining Company following suit in August and December, Mackay looked with satisfaction at the Norcross. Within eight months its daily production had mounted from 100 to 180 tons of ore.

The shrinking days of fall found Mackay directing 187 men in the unloading and storing away of cordwood and timbers for winter use in the "best managed mine on the lead." Fair was superintending the sinking of the main shaft below the 1,100-foot level and running prospecting drifts in the old levels. Necessary repairs required a suspension of dividends, but the stockholders did not worry. The most valuable development on the lead since 1865 was begun on November 20—a drift from the very center of the ore body toward the north boundary of the mine. This resulted a month later in an important strike on the 1,500-foot level. Two thousand dollars a ton, the quartz assayed! Instanter, heat, effective enemy of the mines, called a temporary halt to the frenzied digging.

In spite of this setback, the Norcross' output tripled during the first year. By the end of 1870, it was to be quadrupled, its stock increasing 600 per cent in value in two years. With an additional twelve months, one million dollars in profit was to be the meed for the cluster of Irishmen.

"It was the beginning of all our fortunes," Fair claimed. "We had all the money in that mine that any man could want. We just worked it for its dividends."[8]

8

It was Christmas Eve of 1869. John Mackay paused in the mixing of a new drink of many ingredients, one which had replaced the lemonade and claret punch so favored in the heat of August. Eggnog it was called. But eggnog had to wait, as the Sisters of Charity had come to express their appreciation for the many gifts he had sent them. Formalities over, Mackay returned to sample his drink while he considered the future.

Mrs. Mackay was suffering from a nervous affliction. Rough Virginia was not suited to her high-strung nature. A town that got its excitement from the visit of an homunculus—Commodore Nutt and the Tom Thumb party; the crowd that gathered daily on C Street for the race between the Wells, Fargo buckboard and the Pacific Union Express Company's pony, and the ensuing drink fest; the endless enjoyment of such a "sell" as presenting departing theater troupes with beautifully labeled bottles of salt water, colored with bitters, for quenching their thirst on the long trip across the Sierra—these were not parts of a mode of life Mrs. Mackay wished to live.

Already she was planning a trip to Europe. Her physician had advised consultation with a famous Parisian specialist and relaxation at a Continental health resort. It was not the expense that worried Mackay, since he was considered almost a millionaire, but the prospect of many empty months ahead. Only the knowledge that an heir to his growing business was on the way gave him encouragement. John William, Jr., was born on August 12, 1870, in San Francisco, and not many months later, Marie-Louise and her two children left for Europe. The miner's great love for his family was forced to ride pillion to ambition.

The underground harvest of the Norcross mine had not satisfied expanding John Mackay. Just as Kentuck had been the springboard for his plunge into a pool of wealth, so was Hale & Norcross the pontoon destined to carry him to an ocean of fortune and trouble.

5   Immeasurable Empire

1

John Mackay had maintained, since his early tunneling in Union ground, that the abandoned workings of the Comstock would still reveal quantities of gold and silver. Even if the ore was low-grade, the new machinery and improved system of mining would eliminate much of the former waste, and permit good profits.

How much the following article, written by J. T. Goodman, editor of the *Territorial Enterprise,* might have influenced Mackay will never be known, but it supported his future actions as well as justified his persistent faith in the Bullion mine.

Recent developments seem to have established the correctness of the theory that the great Comstock Lode is limitless in depth, and the cheering effect of the discovery is begun to be observed in every avenue of trade and industry. . . . The lowest depths reached are showing bodies of ore as vast and valuable as were found nearer the surface, and improved machinery . . . will enable ores to be raised and profitably reduced at a depth ten times greater than has yet been obtained.

The Comstock Lode has been traced a distance of over two miles, yet not one-fourth of this length has been worked at all. It abounds in great stretches that appear to be barren. But are they really so?

In formation the Comstock is exceedingly irregular. Like the billows of the ocean, the rich deposits seem to rise and fall, but the opinion is rational that somewhere along the vein, every foot of it, either at the surface or at the depth of hundreds or thousands of feet, valuable ores may be found.

Extending from the Gould & Curry to Ophir, *one of these barren stretches is to be found,* from which but little ore of value has ever been taken. A systematic search is now being made along it, and we are not permitted to doubt that the labor applied and money expended will find abundant reward in the end.

Longitudinal section of the north end of the
Comstock Lode.

| Sierra Nevada 3300' |
| Union Con. 600' |
| Mex 600' |
| Ophir 675' |
| 1310' |
| Best & Belcher 224' |
| Gould & Curry 921' |
| Savage 800' |
| Hale & Norcross 400' |

The history of the 1,310 feet of the lode mentioned in Goodman's final paragraph is an interesting one, considered in the light of its final outcome. At the time of the lead's discovery in 1859, seven different locators seized this section and began to tear into its soil. Hastily removing the few small ore bodies near the surface, they continued digging through barren clay in hopes of deeper deposits. An inflood of water at a depth of three hundred to four hundred feet forced them to suspend operations, and for lack of quick returns, these early prospectors placed their claims on the market at a ridiculously high price.

The mines of Savage, Hale & Norcross, Gould & Curry, etc., offered at low figures, were immediately developed, but this strip adjoining the rich Ophir on the north and the Best & Belcher on the south, lay silent. By the time its owners decided to reduce their price, all the available money in the district had been invested in other mines, and the four-year period of depression in mines and money market made capital hesitant.

Corporations had become the general fashion, since no single individual was willing to handle one of these claims alone. Thus, for years, this strip of ground was worked only the three days per month required to maintain ownership.

The *Enterprise*, however, was not content to see these northern mines idle. Periodically it tried to renew interest in their development. In the fall of 1867 it suggested a feasible course for them to follow:

"Why do not the California, Central, White & Murphy, Dick Sides, and the Best & Belcher form a combination and sink a prospecting shaft to the eastward on a line with the new works of the other leading companies? The companies named own over 1500 feet of ground in the heart of the great lead, yet make not the slightest move toward its development."

No heed being given to this advice, the newspaper continued for two more years to moot the value of this area. Finally, in 1869, four claims—the Central No. 2, Kinney, White & Murphy, and Sides joined their 710 feet into the Consolidated Virginia Mining Company, and entered upon a systematic search for ore.

By Christmas of the following year, they had expended $161,349—in clay. Their shares began to drop in price, and when the February floods of 1871 arrived, Con Virginia stock tumbled to 1⅝, making the mine worth but $18,850 on the market. Further sinking funds were not forthcoming from the disgruntled stockholders, so again development ceased.

With the remaining six hundred feet of the California and Central No. 1 worth even less, the very existence of this section of the Comstock was ignored. W. C. Ralston, organizer of the company, was convinced of its hopelessness. Sharon, too, who had forged ahead to a dictator's position, crisped his pale fingers disdainfully at it. With dissolving interest, the great lode turned to cockfights, ice-skating, and pedro.

2

It was at this time that John Mackay purchased a ticket to Europe. Departing on the eve of June 28, 1871, he hoped to accomplish two things overseas; persuade his family to return to California and promote the interests of the Comstock among the financiers of the Continent. The nine-year-old immigrant of 1840, now forty years of age, passed through a greater New York City, his dream of wealth fulfilled.

Mackay's son, "Willie," was now eleven months old. Mrs. Mackay, however, was not ready to abandon Europe for Nevada with its alternating parching dryness and uncontrollable floods. Why wouldn't John let others handle his business?

"The only sure way I can make a success of mining is to keep my own nose in the ground," he informed her.

She didn't understand that her husband was not content to be an ordinary miner. He intended to be master of the greatest mines in the world! Devoted as he was to his family, the merry and relaxed life of the spas had to be denied.

Now was the time to fight Sharon, because the banker had loaned three of the five million in capital of the Bank of California on undiscovered ore. If these mines played out, every cent invested would be lost.

The volcano of silver and gold was beginning to rumble, and Mackay must be in the front line to measure picks with those who contested his right to the rule of the desert kingdom. On the Comstock a battle was brewing—a battle of the strong against the strong. Mackay was secretly espoused to Virginia, jocund city of unpledged allegiance, of persons at ease only in extremes, whose roughness fitted only one mold —that of courage. Back to boiling swell he sailed alone.

3

Once again Mackay and Fair stood side by side on the long lead, but this time they felt beneath their feet the pulsations of the heart of the mountain. Coming from the distance, as if through fog, sounded the hush-hush of slow, shuffling steps, and the "Hi-o-la-a-lum-a-lum" of the song to "Pah-Ah." The red men were praying for a good crop of pine nuts, and success in fishing and the hunt.

Mackay and Fair wanted success also. To obtain it they were willing to risk their entire fortunes in penetrating a supposed treasure house far beneath the despised surface of those 1,310 feet of acarpous clay. To the north and to the south, the ledges resounded with the thud of picks and shovels. Why should the very core of Mount Davidson remain silent? Its eleven thousand shares were on the market. This might be the chance to capture the sceptre of authority from the Bank of California.

There were many meetings in Flood and O'Brien's office. The firm must buttress its plans well. Three-fourths of the entire stock had to be bought in before control could be announced with safety.

The buying began. Slowly reacting to the sudden stimulus, the shares climbed—$13, $30, $35. On January 11, 1872, the dication of the Consolidated Virginia Mining Company passed to the Mackay firm. Eliot Lord estimated that they paid not more than $50,000 for their stock.

The Comstock greeted the announcement of ownership with a guffaw. Sharon and Ralston indulged in a hearty laugh. So Mackay had boasted he would be owner of the best mines in Nevada! Fair, with his reputation for accuracy, was at last to be shown up as a fake! Why sow the sand when other mines needed that capital to continue development?

Barren ground, the lode called this property. Virgin ground, the enterprising firm whispered, for there was no indication of a break in the fissure, and it was flanked by bonanzas.

How could they have so much confidence, knowing that the abundant Ophir lead had given out on the 600-foot level, and that the Gould & Curry mine, at 1000 feet, had run into unprolific ground? Even the most experienced of Comstock miners considered it "whistling jigs at a milestone" to hunt for deposits below this depth.

"I thought where mines were richest on the surface," Fair said later, "they were liable to be poorest at the bottom, and those containing great quantities of quartz would have the ore further down."[1]

Mackay, meanwhile, laid the important groundwork for future security by hiring a competent lawyer to investigate all titles of the various mines included in his company. Ownership, in many instances not recorded, was difficult to trace, but after some time the attorney reported clear titles to each one. The significance of this would appear in a few years, when over a dozen suits were instituted for part ownership. Now the firm quietly merged the Con Virginia ground with that of the California and Central.

"That was the time to put your hand in your pocket," Fair said, "because we had the stock and we were sinking a deep shaft in the Con."[2]

This shaft, of two compartments, was already down four hundred feet. The small shed over the little donkey engine used for hoisting was inadequate protection against both sun and storm, and had to be replaced by modern buildings and machinery. Work began once more; but this time the men who directed its progress had in their minds an exact picture of the nature of the vein. Behind this data, Mackay and Fair placed their reason, judgment, and faith, in addition to the equally important financial support of Flood and O'Brien in San Francisco's stock market.

Sharon had not been idle in the meanwhile. He had used the four depression years to promote a scheme of connecting the mines with the mills, and both with the Central Pacific Railroad in Reno. His bonanza was the Virginia & Truckee Railroad, known as the crookedest road in the United States. With a descent of 1,600 feet in 13½ miles, the passengers actually traveled around a full circle seventeen times.

Twenty-one miles of track, from Virginia City to Carson, were completed on November 13, 1869—a triumph in engineering for I. E. James. The $500,000 subscribed for its construction by Ormsby and Storey counties, and the $700,000 from the mining companies, were a triumph in hypnotism for William Sharon—a gift of bonds from the citizens, to send the wealth of the mines through the hands of practically the same directorate as the Union Mill and Mining Company.

As the big thirty-two pound gun, "General Grant," blazed a salute from Fort Homestead in honor of Sharon and the end of the wagon haul, the Mackay firm conceived the idea of removing another plum from Sharon's basket.

Nature had not let the mining community forget that she, too, was a worthy opponent. Each winter, many mills were forced to suspend operations until the storms arrived with supplies of snow. During the summer months the amount of water obtained from the tiny rivulets fed by the tunnels was inadequate even for residences. With reasons of drought, and the increase of business establishments, homes, mines, and mills, Sharon and his associates had been asking exorbitant prices for little more than bilge water. Many persons refused to pay the tax and stole from the flumes. Though miles of additional tunnels were dug, and springs all along the range secured for a greater supply, the situation reached an acute stage. The stockholders of the Virginia and Gold Hill Water Company, (a consolidation formed in May, 1862, to insure complete monopoly of the sale of water), had become very tired of complaints, so they decided to offer their stock for sale in 1871.

Immediately the Mackay firm bought control and organized a new Virginia and Gold Hill Water Company, its trustees including W. S. Hobart, president; Walter Dean; and John Skae, a member of the old organization. It was a motley crew of recent rivals.

Johnny Skae, former millionaire gambler, had already taken the position of barometer of mining stocks for James Flood. This sharp-witted fellow, who had gone to Europe and eclipsed the brother of the Sultan at rouge et noir, was worth saving from the consequences of his own recklessness. Known in San Francisco as the perfect stock gambler and leader of the young speculators, penniless Skae proved to be a colorful spot on Mount Davidson's drab face. Loud in dress, with a penchant for wine frappé and pretty actresses, Mackay thought him more refined at heart than he appeared, and pleasant enough. He got along well with the Mackay group.

4

At the same time that the work was going forward in the Con Virginia mine, the new water company called in Hermann Schussler for an important consultation. Schussler was engineer of the Sutro Tunnel project at this time, and destined to become chief engineer for the Spring Valley Water Works of San Francisco in December of 1873. Could water be brought to Washoe, cheaply and effectually, from the slopes of the Sierra? It was a wild scheme, but after the German engineer had surveyed the territory around Lake Tahoe, he said, "Yes."

Marlette Lake, one mile east of Tahoe, was to be eventually the main mountain source of supply; but for the first pipe line, Hobart Creek, in the Sierra Nevada, would be used. The proposed line would have to form an inverted siphon (U) in the Washoe Valley, and Schussler estimated that a pressure of 1,720 feet perpendicular would have to be sustained—a feat never before attempted in the history of water companies.

When San Francisco learned of the plan, it exclaimed, "Impossible!" Still, the new corporation went forward and

bought up the necessary lands around Marlette Lake to prevent the cutting of timber which must act as a snow reservoir, since the real reservoir would not be large enough to
hold the annual supply of water demanded. The experimen-
ters then built a long flume from Hobart Creek—twenty-one
miles in a straight line from Virginia—to a spur 1,950 feet
above Washoe Valley. There connections with an iron pipe
line conducted the water to the valley floor, across its basin
to the opposite precipitous wall, where again it had to be
raised 1,496 feet to the level of the Washoe Range.

On August 1, 1873, five months after the commencement
of the project, all those who for years had cursed roundly the
rates, the hardness, the alkali and bugs of the local water,
were told to gather for the arrival of Sierra water. It was an
impatient, noisy crowd that stared at the mountain to see the
signal fire that would be set off when the water left the flume
and entered the pipe line. Firecrackers, cannons, and pyres of
wood were made ready to welcome it.

At last the warning fire blazed high. One by one the
twenty-six air cocks for the release of air screamed that the
water was racing along the line. A final shriek from the last
air cock preceded the flood of water. Into the dry bed of
Bullion Creek it foamed, heavily loaded with bran and saw-
dust to fill up cracks in the wooden flume. The stream soon
became clear and the townspeople rushed in to taste it. Pure,
cold water in Virginia! Two million gallons a day! Water
from distant Tahoe with the greatest pressure in the world! It
was a triumph in experimental hydraulics.

Mackay turned his attention back to the mines. Fair stepped
forward to take all the credit for the engineering exploit.

An unbiased criticism of James Fair, written by a contemporary, has this to say regarding the affair:

Fair tells me in very positive terms that he . . . was the man to
conceive, to put into execution, and to complete the entire matter,
in opposition to the engineers of the world, so far as their ideas
could be gotten at . . . that Mr. Schussler was simply an instrument
in his hands—a very good man, a very valuable man, but in a side
remark (Fair) says, "I am one of those modest men that don't like
to take credit to myself."
Fair also suggests that Mackay doesn't want the cost of the
Virginia and Gold Hill Water Works given in anything that may
be written about them, but gives no reason for this. I judge, however, that his reason is . . . the works cost so very much less than
the papers have stated it.

They gave out that the works cost two million of money. The object in making the statement was to cause the people to quietly pay the very exorbitant water rates. And I suppose that Fair is the one, and not Mackay, that doesn't want it spoken of, but he uses Mackay as a scapegoat in this instance.[3]

It will not be long before Fair's nickname is "Slippery Jim."

5

Ambitious William Sharon had not been idle while his rivals were forging ahead. By the end of 1872 he had impaled seventeen of the Comstock's twenty-four mills on the spear of the Union Mill and Mining Company, had developed a great timber flume industry, and, with spies in all the mines watching for those with the widest streak of fat, he hoped to get more mines to keep his many mills running.

Only the unexpected seizure of the Crown Point mine in 1871 by Alvinza Hayward and John P. Jones, members of the bank crowd, had interrupted the smooth running of the syndicate. These seceders formed the Nevada Mill and Mining Company, and with the other antagonistic interests—the Mackay firm, Sutro, and the grumbling State of Nevada, were causing a worried frown to appear on the complacent faces of Ralston and Sharon.

However, a new move on the part of the Mackay clique took away its temporary threat. The addition of the Gould & Curry, a mine long in *borrasca,* to Mackay's unproductive Bullion and Fair's poor Savage mine, appeared nothing short of ridiculous. The Kentuck mine had ceased to pay dividends; the Hale & Norcross, though paying a five-dollar dividend on a daily yield of from 175 to 225 tons, continued to be of poor grade.

With four exhausted claims, and a fifth to be added, this company of hotspurs was lonely in its self-confidence. It was a four-man team now, as Walker had withdrawn in 1869. Dissatisved with the firm's apparent recklessness, he had accepted Mackay's ready offer of three million dollars for his interest. With six-sixteenths, or approximately twice as much as each of the other three, Mackay had undisputed leadership of the group.

6

The purpose behind the control of the Gould & Curry was to have a place from which to run a drift through the Best & Belcher into the Con Virginia section. The vertical shaft then being dug in the latter would connect with the Curry drift made from the 1,200-foot level. Mackay and Fair agreed to develop the southern half of the claim first, leaving the California ground adjoining the Ophir for future prospecting.

Throughout 1872 the waste rock being removed from the Con Virginia showed that the shaft was lengthening. Simultaneously, the great drift progressing horizontally to meet it had crossed the boundary into the Best & Belcher. Two hundred thousand dollars had made its trail. Flood warned the pair of miners that the independent stockholders were vigorously protesting further assessments. It appeared as if they were pouring water into the broken cistern of the Danaïdes. From the surface, one could not realize the enormous amount of capital required to keep continuous shifts of men at work and a constant flow of supplies going into the earth.

Superintendent Fair and Assistant Mackay maintained that they were on the trail of the vein, because the hanging wall and the footwall persisted. This meant nothing to the small shareholders, who promptly began to dump their stock on the market. Flood and O'Brien bought more of it, and the four speculators continued to assess themselves without a falter.

Greater speed! ordered Fair, as the workmen headed north for the Con Virginia. More miners! Mackay insisted. Only one hundred feet farther to the boundary of this mine.

Mackay decided that, with a bonanza not far off, he would hurry to Europe for a visit. If they hit it rich, it might be a long time before he would be able to leave again. Off he went, exchanging the heat and stifling air of dark and dripping galleries for happy months at world-famous watering places, accompanied by a charming wife, a prattling, two-year-old son, and a stepdaughter who had already developed Continental mannerisms.

James Fair, left behind to handle the gigantic task alone, overexerted himself by untold hours in the ground. Why wasn't John here to relieve him? Of all times, this was when he should be attending to business! Fair became seriously ill and cabled his partner to return. Perhaps one day Mackay would have to decide who was his legitimate spouse—Louisa or the channel of silver and gold.

On January 23, 1873, the *Gold Hill News* informed the lode that "John W. Mackay, of mining and stock combination, returned after an extended tour of several months sight-seeing and visiting in Europe. He left his family enjoying the beautiful city of Nice ... and returns to the happy land of sagebrush, looking nice himself and evidently much rejuvenated by his trip."

The old miners of Virginia continued to ridicule the outcome of the Con Virginia enterprise, and though temptation to throw it up was strong, Mackay and Fair were as stubborn as the stone-layers they followed. What did they care if the valuation of the mines was decreasing? They were not interested in stocks. The eyes of the lode could not follow the movements of this new wheel of men, whose sweeping revolutions blurred before those who looked only at the present. The ground appeared very unsteady beneath the corporate feet of the Mackay firm.

7

It was February, and the drift had crossed into Con Virginia territory. The eyes of the ferrets were temporarily switched to their brains to determine the future course. One hundred feet they went over the boundary—150—166. There in the labyrinth of heat and water, the thud of unprolific clay was replaced by the ring of quartz. Fair was beside himself with excitement. Hurry! Hurry! Eleven feet more and a seven-foot vein of ore was exposed. James Fair removed a chunk and brought it to the surface.

"How much would you say it assays, John?"

"At least sixty dollars a ton."

"That will be forty dollars net. My boy, we'll say nothing of this yet. We'll remove the ore through the old Bonner shaft, until we're more certain of the outcome."

For all their calmness, there was a sudden sag in the muscles that hungered for sleep, and in the nerves stretched to the breaking point. The firing of the guns could wait.

Assessments were at an end. By the first of March, three shifts were removing twenty-five tons of ore daily from the twelve-foot vein on the 1,167-foot level. Prospecting still went on as a cut across the vein and extending along either side was ordered. This disclosed many small bodies of ore. It could mean but one thing—the main vein was widening in the shape of a V!

8

"The Con Virginia shaft bids fair to be soon on the paying dividend list," reported the *Gold Hill News,* but the statement aroused no interest. Other mines were attracting general attention: Belcher was paying four and five dollars a share each month; Chollar-Potosi, Hale & Norcross, Crown Point, and Belcher were shipping ninety-five carloads of ore each day over Sharon's railroad. What did the Comstock care about twenty-five tons a day from this other mine? Even Sharon ignored it, his thoughts occupied with Hayward and Jones, who had just added the Justice mine to their control.

Floods closed up the Con Virginia drifts, causing entire weeks to be lost in reopening and retimbering them. During the night, the mighty weight of the mountain pressed close the sides of the tunnels. This granary of nature was extravagantly protected. Yet, on the miners dug, fighting every obstacle of nature with all the known weapons of man.

At six in the morning, Fair and Mackay trudged up the lode in their rough miners' clothes. Day and night they pushed forward the work of excavating the main shaft, which, now 710 feet deep, had still some distance to go before it connected with the Curry drift and the ore body. The air had become increasingly foul in spite of the powerful blowers which sent down a constant supply of fresh air. Two hundred and fifty feet further along, the great drift was to strike the Con Virginia shaft. It was October before the connection was made. Then the strong current of air cleared the mines of its stifling fumes and made work easier. Henceforth all ore was raised through the main shaft.

Five hundred thousand dollars had been expended in prospecting, but by March the vein had grown to forty feet in width. How great its actual size was, neither Mackay nor Fair dared to say. October found them "breasting out."

Muscular, pale-skinned workmen, stripped to their waists, excavated a chamber twenty feet high and fifty-four feet wide. Sides, top, and floor were all in the ore vein. The invaders, looking through the square-sets of supporting timbers, saw crystals of iron, crystals of quartz—blue and white and purple. The cavern glistened with the black lustrous "silver-glance," and sparkled with the green and gray of chloride silver ore and the delicate copper pyrites.

When Mackay assayed samples of this ore, he was astounded—$90 to $632 a ton! But more stock, Flood and O'Brien!

That month and the next, the mine was worked with a zeal and discipline unknown to mining history. Two hundred tons of bullion a day were being hoisted—$250,000 a month! It had come just in time, for the Norcross, yielding only forty tons of low-grade ore daily, was forced to levy a five-dollar assessment in January to keep the mine open.

9

What was the matter with the lode? Was it the steady progress of the work that had fooled everyone, including William Sharon? Was it the belief that the gigantic energies expended in the Con Virginia were merely exploratory? Or was it the fact that Mackay and Fair were not interested at this time in stimulating the stock market? Why was there such apathy among the speculators?

This ever-widening stream of metal, 700 feet deep and 1,300 feet long, was causing no more excitement than an ordinary strike. Didn't the Comstock realize that the roof was off the greatest storehouse of wealth in the world, where nature had been adding bit by bit, jewel by jewel, increasing and ever elaborating her hidden hoard? This was the Big Bonanza of the century!

It was Adolph Sutro who had stolen the limelight with his tunnel project. The newspapers which had hailed him as a benefactor of the mining community when he began the project in 1866, now called him a "crack-brained enthusiast," a "tunnel maniac."

Sutro's plan was to dig a tunnel at the foot of the mountain, directly across all the ore bodies, and thus provide a drain for the entire lode. Pumping water out of the mines was costly, as the engines were fired with wood.

Sutro had obtained the support of both Federal and state governments, some thirty mines, and the Bank of California in 1866 on the arguments that his tunnel would give impetus to the exploration of the mines north of the Gould & Curry, and permit inexpensive extraction of an immense amount of low-grade bullion lying waste in all the mines due to the great cost of handling it below two hundred feet.

Now when Mackay and Fair were opening the Big Bonanza, New York capitalists nullified their pledges of support to Sutro, and the Bank of California cancelled all subscriptions to the tunnel fund of the mining companies under its power. Senators, legislators, merchants, and miners were condemning the entire project. One amazing story after another of Sutro's attempts to raise five million dollars for the continuance of his work occupied the front columns of the press and captured the interest of the dark mountain.

10

James Fair departed for the Atlantic states the first of the year, 1874, but returned February 19. The way Mackay did things never satisfied him. Fair had a peculiar way of handling his business. Virginia became more aware of this as a news story broke into print:

At a time when a certain cross cut in the Con Virginia, showing very rich ore, was made, Fair went down the shaft about midnight and found two miners in the main drift cooling off.

"My son," said Fair, picking up a piece of rock that had fallen from a car from the cross-cut, and addressing one of the men, "My son, what do you think that rock is worth?"

"It won't pay for crushing," answered the judicious miner.

"What do you think, my son?" asked Fair, turning to the other.

The man, anxious to display his knowledge, blurted out, "It's worth $2000 a ton if it's worth a cent."

"You're a miner," said Fair approvingly; and five minutes after, when he went on top, he ordered the foreman to discharge the second speaker on the grounds that "he knew too damn much."[4]

The innocent questions of "Slippery Jim" would ever be veiled with subtle purpose. He knew just how to play with a man's eagerness. Fair always listened with flattering attention to what a person had to say, but concealed his feelings completely by belittling himself until the speaker had told him what he wanted to hear.

"Nothing with Fair is done by direction," a contemporary biographer of the superintendent claimed. "It is all by indirection and a good deal of palaver ... very hearty, he figuratively puts his arms around you."[5]

But this perfect dissimulation, to which he invariably took recourse, was imperceptibly twisting the original man into an amazing pattern.

11

The first dividend from the Con Virginia, three dollars a share, was declared in May of 1874. Up to this time the owners had turned back every cent into the exploration of the mine. The systematic search still continued, however.

From the 1,000- to the 1,200-, 1,300-, and 1,400-foot levels the work went on. Drifts running lengthwise, winzes perforating level after level for ventilation and ore chutes, crosscuts at every turn, tunnels and more tunnels, all telling the same story—a mass of wealth averaging 40 feet in width, in places as broad as 320 feet. One crib of timber after another was added to support the cavities, until the inner mountain was a wooden honeycomb. The main drifts were roomy, with good air compression from two blowers on the surface.

Mackay tried out the Burleigh rock drill in the Con Virginia and was enthusiastic over the new invention.

"No man is more ready to adopt improvements," was Dan De Quille's opinion of Mackay. "He is ever ready to spend money for labor-saving machinery. Those of his men who imagine they have discovered a new plan of doing any kind of work, whereby a saving in time or muscle can be affected, always find an attentive listener in Mackay, and all encouragement.

"He frequently stimulates their inventive faculties by telling them of certain things for which he desires some new mode of working to be thought out, or some new machine to be constructed."[6]

New improvements not found in other mines continued to appear in the Con Virginia. There was constructed an air chimney 5 by 9 feet, extending 25 feet above the shaft building, to relieve the mine of the immense amount of steam in the huge underground workings.

Mackay and Fair were familiar with every detail. Each of the 424 workmen was excellent. The company's assay office boasted two of the most competent men in the West—Ross and Wheeler, formerly of the United States Mint.

Before the close of 1873, the directors of the Con Virginia Mining Company, presided over by Edward Barron of the water company, had met to form a new corporation—the California Mining Company. It comprised the former California, Kinney, and Central No. 1 and No. 2 mines. Though work in this ground would not be attempted for some time, everything was put in order.

With the Big Bonanza in sight, the Mackay team incorporated also the Pacific Mill and Mining Company. Mr. Barron, later replaced by Mr. Wallace, made the fifth trustee.

12

The production of the Con Virginia mounted in November of 1874 to four hundred tons a day. By Christmas when the

1,500-foot level was reached, the gleaming ore body was fully exposed.

Fair was now ready for a dramatic play. He had been irritated for some time by the attitude of the San Francisco newspapers regarding the value of the great mine.

He sought out Dan De Quille at the *Enterprise* office and told him to go through the mine and write his own story. Dan had an enviable reputation for accuracy in mining statements.

"Make your own estimates, so they can't say I told you," Fair advised him.

Thus Dan De Quille was the first outsider to view "The Heart of the Comstock," as he headlined his story. One hundred and sixteen million dollars was his estimate! The world gasped.

Philipp Deidesheimer, inventor of the square-set, and miner of twenty years' experience, read the article and hurried to Virginia City to voice his opinion.

"One billion, five hundred million dollars is the valuation of each mine!" he reported. "It can pay five thousand dollars a share if properly managed."

Three billion for the two mines! Deidesheimer's statement was to bring ill-fated results, both for him and others.

Now the people turned to John Mackay. Here was a miner of unsurpassed judgment, who would tell them the truth. They received a typical Mackay answer.

"I do not wish to make an estimate. I prefer to mine it out, and then take the milling returns."

But surely a general idea——

"It is ridiculous to make any statement," he declared, "for there are many elements that can destroy the most careful calculations. When do we know what moment we'll strike a barren mass of rock, a wall of porphyry, or horses within a vein?"

Still the public cried for estimates, exaggerations if necessary. They got them. Mr. H. A. Linderman of the United States Mint came from Carson City with his assistants. For hours he measured and figured before reporting that "with proper allowances, the ore body equals an amount, which, taken at the actual assays, will give as the ultimate yield of the two mines, three hundred million dollars."

Five or six million dollars was the average estimate of this imperial treasure, and anyone who said less was looked upon with disfavor. Valued at from ten thousand to twelve thousand dollars a running inch, the blood of the Comstock raced through hot brains.

Dr. Brennan, lecturing to the lode not to "lace too tight nor get too tight," carried little weight as the speculative mania revived. With values soaring hourly, in a short time there was not enough gold in America to buy control of the Comstock. Every barren place on the lode was now considered to contain a bonanza below the 1,000-foot level. The mines adjoining the Big Bonanza rose fastest of all. By January, Ophir was rated at $31,000,000, Best & Belcher, $9,-000,000, Mex the same, and the rest varied from $3,000,000 to $20,000,000 each.

Con Virginia shares, worth $1.00 in July of 1870, rose to $15 in June of 1872, $115 in March of 1873, $176 in November of 1874, and in January of 1875 were $700 apiece, making the total valuation of the mine $75,600,000. The California mine, not developed until late in 1874, had risen from $37 a share at that time, to $780. Its paper valuation was $84,240,000—rated higher because "the big bulge of the Big Bonanza seemed to be principally in the California ground."[7]

Thus, in five years, the 1,310 feet of ground, bought at $50,000, had increased in reputed value to more than $150,-000,000. It was deemed advisable to increase the 10,700 shares of the Con Virginia to 108,000. The Bonanza Kings owned 60,000 of this amount. The California stock was simultaneously increased to 540,000 shares, with possession of 300,000 in the hands of Mackay, Fair, Flood, and O'Brien.

This mine was a mass of porphyry, burdened with crystals of stephanite, clusters of pure silver, coiled wires of dark sulphurets, and "nests" of wire gold. From the California would come the most beautiful specimens now possessed by collectors.

The Bonanza ore was so rich that it was sent to the mills just as it was dug out, and worked without assorting. At times, waste rock or low-grade ore was added to make it easier to handle, and to prevent considerable waste. The thrilling words—stopes, lodes, drifts, and bonanzas, heard in Flood and O'Brien's bar, at last had meaning to John Mackay.

13

In the magnificence of this dark vault beneath simple-hearted Washoe, men in blue cotton or thin woolen overalls, gray or blue woolen shirts, and caps or felt hats, ascended and descended in the crowded cages. Everywhere men were at work, building in a forest of wooden props to support the

swelling and shrinking clay and feldspar walls, picking away
in hot drifts, placing powder to blast the rocks from the
breasts, loading the cars and shoving them along the narrow
tracks to the station on that level, holding power drills amid
smoke and gas filtering through the dark galleries—all forming the wondorous music of the lode. The mountain was no
longer silent. Tumultuous days of excitement, expectancy,
and singular charm were here.

John Mackay arose at 5:00 A.M. to be at the mines at six.

His inspection tour included a critical survey of the framework, for the ever-present heat and moisture rotted and
weakened the timbers, and permitted the ground to shift and
crumble. He had a horror of mine disasters, and it wasn't
only cave-ins that worried him. Many a night he left his bed
to pull on the heavy, clay-smeared brogans, overalls, loose
shirt and hat, and rush out into the darkness to the mines.
Anxiously he followed the drifts, sniffing to detect the
slightest odor of burning wood, watching for scurrying rats
that warned of caving ground.

He took extraordinary precautions to prevent fire because,
if such should ever start in the continuous network of lumber,
nothing on earth could extinguish its slow, devastating progress. Only well-placed bulkheads could check its advance. The
closing of these two mines for countless years would mean financial ruin for their investors, and perhaps some loss of life.

One winter night in 1874, when Mackay headed toward
the Con Virginia shaft, his worst fears appeared to be realized. Columns of flame were flaring up against the dark sky.
Other men joined him in hurrying to the mine. Drawing near,
they saw a white flame shooting from the abandoned Ophir
shaft. Like the fingers of a spread hand, the glaring rays
streamed far into the night sky. There was an accompanying
sweet, sickening smell that definitely was not burning timber.
Phosphurated gas it was, the belch of decaying fungi that had
formed on crushed timbers.

Mackay went to his mine with sickening heart. Such would
eventually be the fate of the Con Virginia shaft with its tough
Sierra pines—a breeding ground for the deadly firedamp.

6   Refocusing the Lens

1

Mrs. Mackay had returned to California in the spring of 1873, a few months after her husband. She had established herself at 825 O'Farrell Street in San Francisco, and set out to win the elusive Crockers, Huntingtons, and Stanfords as determinedly as her husband was pursuing the thread of gold.

Seamstress and washerwoman from a mining camp, married to a miner, a common laborer, she could not gain entree into this social clique of aristocrats, who continued to look upon her as a *parvenue*.

In spite of their indifference, Mrs. Mackay preferred fashionable Montgomery Street with its exclusive shops to Virginia's C Street, garbed in no particular style, where, in passing its dirty stores, a broomful of dust was likely to be swept into one's face.

The city of Virginia, with its jargon, could never be home to her again. The lengthy processions of quartz teams that wended their slow way from mines to mills, the Chinese hawking wood by the donkey-back load, and the Indian women strolling with papooses closely ensconced in willow baskets were not picturesque scenes to this strange daughter of a pioneer.

If her husband desired he could spend his time on the lode, where wet clay and candle grease made him one of the crowd. She knew that the discovery of the Big Bonanza contained no element of chance. He had worked hard in Virginia City and now, with unbelievable success his, he enjoyed walking down its sloping streets in the evening, listening to the music of piano or fiddle from the beer saloons as it mingled with the whirr of heavy machinery at the hoisting works and the clatter of the mill stamps. This was his world of Atlas types, a jangling world of incessant bustle, of smoke and steam, of dirt and dreams.

For Mackay there was a wonderful compensation for the social failure of his wife in San Francisco. A second son, Clarence, was born on April 17, 1874. Thoroughly middle class in motives, the father clung stubbornly to his family.

"He's a solid man, like John Mackay," was a remark often heard on the lode in 1875. It had replaced the expression of the early seventies, "He is way up," and was preferred to "He's too tall," in the new repertoire of slang signifying approbation.

John Mackay was trying to retain his individuality as earnestly as Joaquin Miller, who, though he had had his long hair cut in London, preserved his poetical idiosyncrasies by donning green pantaloons. For Mackay to remain simple and unaffected while surrounded by countless flatterers would not be as easy as he thought. As the great spring of his inner nature slowly compressed under the weight of his increasing fortune, unassuming Washoe helped him maintain a solid stance.

"Today he walks about the streets of Virginia City as cordial as in the old days," a January, 1875, *San Francisco Chronicle* said of Mackay, "dresses no better than an ordinary gent in Virginia, eats no better food than a conscientious editor ought to have, and yet so rich that he could, unaided, go down and open at his own expense the Darien Canal, could endow a college in each state of the Union with two million dollars each, or build a double-track, narrow-gauge railroad from San Francisco to New York and solve the problem of cheap transportation."

The *Chronicle*, soon to become an enemy of the Bonanza firm, was supporting it at this time:

Many poor have reaped benefits from the new bonanza. Instead of its managers seeking to gobble it up for themselves, there was not only no secret of its discovery but they actually advised the poor to buy.

They are new men outside the old money ring. It looked at one time as though some half dozen of the most unscrupulous men were, by the squeezing process, to get all the mines, and through them and the speculating mania of the citizens, to get all the lands and lots in San Francisco—a moneyed monopoly dangerous from greed and power. The new enterprise scatters the benefits and assures San Francisco that it is no longer at the mercy of the old junta of mining sharps and money grabbers.

Though William Sharon had lost favor in the bay region, his popularity had increased in Virginia. At the annual celebration of the pioneer society in October, Sharon was elected a life member of the organization, and the old-timers cheered him for several minutes. Under fire, the bank agent had a way with men, too.

Though Mackay and he had been paraded as enemies, the two joined Mr. Mills in the purchase of the *Territorial Enterprise* when J. T. Goodman relinquished ownership in 1873. The new editor was Rollin M. Daggett, and his assistant was C. C. Goodwin, both friends of Mackay.

All was peaceful on the lode. Sharon was installing his new son-in-law, Frank G. Newlands, in his own Sutter Street mansion with a million-dollar dowry on his daughter; Honorable J.P. Jones was on a honeymoon; James Fair was experimenting with a telegraph line to the lower levels of the Con Virginia; Mackay was commuting between his residence on the corner of Howard and Taylor in Virginia and his San Francisco residence. Only Adolph Sutro was repeating his troubles with the bank ring, the railroad, the corporations, and a government that declared he had failed to keep his contract with them.

2

"The Bonanza is undisputably the greatest mass of silver ore ever discovered in any place in the world," Mackay declared to reporter Dan De Quille. "We have not yet fairly started in upon the California. It will require steady work for six months to show what that mine really is.

"In regard to the Con Virginia, some think that the stock has already sold for more than it is worth. The truth is, that it has never sold for one-half of its value; but all this will be seen in good time. Ten years from now, people will all know and admit this. When all our arrangements for working the Con Virginia and California mines are completed, it will begin to be seen."[1]

Among the arrangements Mackay had in mind was the new and powerful hoisting works at the California & Consolidated Virginia shaft which were to be the heaviest and most complete in the state. By means of drifts run into the Con Virginia and California, the C. & C. was to be the main extraction shaft for the two mines.

Sharon had been unable to invest in the Big Bonanza. He

intended to get his profit from it indirectly by building a branch track of the Virginia & Truckee Railroad to the shaft and then charge enormous freight rates on lumber and supplies, and on the shipments of ores to the outside mills.

With characteristic thoroughness Mackay turned from the mines themselves to the saving of their tailings. Down the hill from the Con Virginia and California he had walls of dirt raised about two large excavations. With a continuous flow of waste into them, they soon became blue lakes of liquid debris and pulverized ore. He hoped that the residue of silver might be extracted when the sun had dried the tailings. Little did John Mackay foresee that sixty-three years from this time this refuse was to be worked again with profit, since not even he could harvest it completely.

With the bonanza mines yielding from three hundred to four hundred tons of good ore daily, the stock market vaulted. Once again stores and saloons were crowded, actors played to filled seats, and money circulated freely. Six mines were under the corporate thumb of his firm as Mackay outlined seven more for subdual in the future.

3

While the master miner was occupied with these plans, the "bears" got the better of the "bulls" on Pine Street, San Francisco. Denying the extent of the Big Bonanza, starting all sorts of rumors, they created a panic which put the two mines in scandal.

As recklessly as the people had bought, they cast their stocks on the market at foolish sacrifices. Deidesheimer, who had invested every cent he had to show his faith in his own estimate of the treasure, was but one of the scapegoats at this time.

What difference did it make that John Mackay cried, "There is enough ore in sight to hoist five hundred tons a day for five years from the Con Virginia alone!"

The whispering campaign of *borrasca* grew to a wild cry. Though the Big Bonanza was capable of producing $100,000 in bullion every day, by March 26 Con Virginia shares had dropped from $700 to $420 and California shares from $780 to $84. The lode decreased in value $386,000,000! Every mine on the exchange was reduced from 50 per cent to 250 per cent in valuation.

Just as thousands had been made wealthy by the great

lead, so were an equal number now impoverished. No longer was the control of the leading mines in the hands of the Big Four. Stock manipulators had taken charge of them, making fortunes that now rule the world, ruining business houses which might have become powers. The Comstock stood on tiptoe and dared not breathe.

With barkeepers idle, hotel owners and faro dealers filing petitions for bankruptcy, and creditors wearing sackcloth and ashes, Mackay and his associates were roundly cursed. The accusation was that they had deliberately spread rumors in San Francisco that the mines were played out in order to lower prices and buy in more stock. There could be little truth in this, for a high market at this time would have been more to their advantage.

" 'Speaking of the great crash in stocks,' Mackay told Dan De Quille, 'it is no affair of mine. *My business is mining—* legitimate mining. I see that my men do their work properly in the mines, and that all goes on as it should in the mills. I make my money out of the ore.

" 'Had I desired to do so, I could have gone down to San Francisco with ten thousand shares of stock in my pocket, and by throwing it on the market at the critical moment, I could have brought on a panic and a crash just as had been done.

" 'Suppose I had done so, and had made five hundred thousand by the job—what is that to me? By attending to my legitimate business here at home, I take out five hundred thousand in one week.' "[2]

"In short," Dan De Quille said at this time, "Mackay appears to trouble his head but very little with the ups and downs of stocks, or with the wire-pulling of the stock manipulators. He wants to make no money by engineering crashes in stocks, which ruin thousands upon thousands of industrious and worthy persons.

"During our short conversation, Mackay repeatedly said: 'My business is square, legitimate mining. Here and in San Francisco, persons are constantly coming to me and writing to me to ask: "What shall I buy?" I said to all that came: "Go and put your money in a savings bank." '

"Here Mackay indulged in a quiet laugh as he said, 'You should have seen those folks stare at me. They evidently thought I was a very strange kind of a mining man. But I meant just what I said, and my advice was good. I never advise people to buy mining stock of any kind.'

"Mackay is right in this, as he can never know what jobs may be put up by the stock sharps to break down the price of almost any stock on the list, merit or no merit. By giving no advice, he escapes all reproach and pursues the even tenor of his way, digging his money out of his mines, regardless of all ups and downs and crashes in stocks."

Other members of the Bonanza firm were not so scrupulous. Flood had formed a pool to manipulate and gain control of Savage stocks; Fair was suspected of the best and of the worst.

"In mining matters, many men have received many points from him, while others claim to have been fearfully bitten by his advice," stated the *San Francisco Mail*, with reference to James Fair. "No doubt, like most men, he has friends to support and reward, and enemies to punish."

4

John Mackay was confined to the house the middle of February with gout and rheumatism. However, by using frequent applications of arnica, he was able to return to work within a few days.

In spite of widespread melancholy on the lode, he was jubilant since the Con Virginia mine could pay a three-dollar dividend that month, with the market at its lowest, and expected to issue the same dividend in March. This aided considerably in restoring the colorful and exciting life of the Comstock.

Former Senator William Stewart was back on a visit, surprising all who thought he was becoming old by executing with abandon the intricate movements of the quadrille. Adolph Sutro had returned from Washington, his wagon of baggage causing no little interest in Dayton when a local policeman pursued it on the livery stable's fastest horse, expecting to arrest a peddler dealing out wares without a license. Only amusing Dan De Quille was gone. He was in the East writing his *History of the Big Bonanza*.

New twenty-cent pieces arrived on the Comstock at the same time as a carload of equally intriguing machinery for the C. & C. shaft. The California Mill in Six Mile Canyon was completed in April to take some of the burden from the Con Virginia and small Mariposa mills. One hundred and twenty men were given employment here, and hundreds more in the firm's latest enterprise—the Pacific Wood, Lumber, and Flume Company, incorporated to compete with the Union wood and flume business of the Bank of California.

An unfailing source of lumber was required to furnish eighteen million feet annually in the company's mines, and forty thousand cords of wood in the furnaces which drove the vast machinery. Mackay insisted upon a great store of wood to forestall any attempt at a corner.

Toward this end, the company purchased twelve thousand acres of wooded land between Lake Tahoe and Washoe Valley. Twenty-seven miles of flumes were built, and a small army of woodmen hired to chop the trees that floated to Sharon's railroad. Everything was done on a gigantic scale as John Mackay stepped forward to a more secure position on the naked hills of Washoe.

5

The two mine managers were beginning to tangle. Every time Fair went to San Francisco for a rest of two or three weeks, Mackay hired more men at the mines. Returning, Fair as promptly fired them. The effect upon the workmen was a rally to the support of Mackay, and a thumb-to-nose fluttering of the fingers at "Slippery Jim's" back. Any story to Fair's discredit suited their risibilities, and was deemed worthy of frequent repetition.

On April 11, Mackay and Deidesheimer took the train for San Francisco, as Fair was back after a visit to the bay region. The following day, the *Gold Hill News* printed this "rich joke on a superintendent, who boasts that if he is posted on anything, it is on iron work." There was no doubt left in the reader's mind as to who was the butt of the story, since Fair constantly bragged of his ability as a machinist and his genius for invention.

"Everybody who knows anything about making a miner's pick, is aware that the iron part with a hole in the middle is made first, and that the steel points are welded on afterward.

"Said superintendent returned from San Francisco from a visit of two to three weeks, and on arriving at the mine, at once began to inspect the premises to see that everything was right. He entered the blacksmith shop, looked around for a few minutes, then went into the office, called the clerk and ordered the blacksmith paid off and discharged.

"The blacksmith took his money and went off without

saying a word, knowing he could easily get work elsewhere. The foreman soon after arrived, and missing the blacksmith, who was a first class workman, asked the clerk where he was. The latter replied that the superintendent had discharged him.

"The foreman then found the superintendent and said, 'What did you discharge the blacksmith for?'

" 'Because he is of no-account.'

" 'He is the best workman we ever had.'

" 'No, he isn't. I saw him making picks. He makes every one of them too short, and I caught him lengthening them out!' "

There were claws and teeth beneath the still watchfulness of the short-necked, broad-shouldered superintendent. Superbly conscious of his own cleverness, Fair gave the impression of being always amused at the antics of others. Knowing that he could play a while with his victim before crushing him, he remained complacent, facile, and detached. He was charming on acquaintance, a master of tact with tongue coiled in his cheek.

No tourist visiting the mines appeared to be a bore to him. He would place his hand on the shoulder of a too-inquisitive stranger and remark with an engaging smile, "My son, would it be too much to ask you to come around tomorrow? These mines are any amount of trouble to me, and business, you know, makes imperative demands upon one's time."

The tourist would oblige Fair, but upon his return the following day he would be unable to see the superintendent. The clerk had been instructed, "If that idiot comes again, tell him I'm not here!"[3]

Reverence of James Fair sprang from his personal magnetism, but, at the same time, his smooth-lipped confidence was breeding distrust.

6

The following incident, occurring in June of 1875, illustrates the attitude of the miners regarding "Boss" Mackay.

"Mackay bet me a hundred dollar suit of clothes, that I could not remove from the fifteen-hundred-foot level six hundred tons of ore a day for a month," Hugh Lamb, foreman of the Con Virginia mine related. "I took the bet, told my men what I had done, and set them to work. They were as anxious to make a record as I was—the bet was nothing—and they worked like devils."[4]

They made the record, averaging 633 tons a day. The foreman got his hundred-dollar outfit, while Mackay continued to wear a twenty-five-dollar suit.

"The Brains," as Mackay was known, worked by influence rather than audible direction. Though his glance and speech were imperious, his gestures and actions betrayed his simplicity. The miners knew that fustian phrases were not suited to him. Therefore, when Virginia began to distribute chevrons and cordons with the same recklessness shown in speculation, the rich miner received no military title.

A man worth twenty-five thousand dollars was dubbed "Captain." "Major" was bestowed on individuals possessing fifty thousand dollars. Though Fair deserved the title of "General" in accordance with this scale, "Colonel" was his appellation, for it had been given him when he was worth one hundred thousand dollars.

"Boss of the Comstock—Prince of Miners," Dan De Quille called Mackay. This was more to his liking than the designation "Bonanza King."

"That 'Bonanza King' is stuff," he told Eliot Lord one day when the two men were tramping through the hot drifts of the Con Virginia mine. "It makes nothing of me but a millionaire with a swelled head."[5]

Wealth was no longer the distinction he sought. He was hunting for the excitement of the hunt, for the joy of another victory, and the satisfaction of beating the best.

His thrills came, not from being designated a millionaire, but from his ability to increase Bonanza dividends to ten dollars a share, from knowing that at last foreign capitalists were taking notice of his mines, from such little things as the authority to say to the workmen, "It's such fine weather, all those who want to go picnicking have the day off."

The mixture of aggressiveness and self-restraint, of hotheadedness and hardheadedness in John Mackay, had resulted from a conflict between his hankering for distinction and his contempt for being known to like being known.

Virginia City and Gold Hill, populated by nearly twenty thousand persons, turned to John Mackay as the new power of the Comstock. He was their "Chief."

Amid this new glory came a foreboding of disaster. Scarcity of water closed up the great Con Virginia mill which had been so proud of its forty gas burners. If the water company did not hurry in meeting the increased requirements, nature might yet demand her hecatombs from this greedy kingdom—unified by a single thought, more gold and more silver!

7

Persons stepping out for a clove between acts at Piper's Opera House on the evening of August 26, 1875, were surrounded by the customary group of boys at the entrance begging for money. When one gentleman offered a check on the Bank of California, he was refused with the statement, "No sir, it's played out!"

"Played out!" the bewildered cry echoed across the lode.

The next morning the entire West was informed of the bank's difficulties—a catastrophe that closed not only its own doors, but those of many San Francisco banks.

Were the mines to blame? Apparently not, since the amount of money withdrawn for speculative purposes had not been great enough to cause this disaster. But a defalcation of $3,000,000 to $3,500,000 in assets abstracted from the bank without the knowledge of its directors, plus one million loaned to irresponsible parties, this in addition to the stringency of the money market in San Francisco caused by a heavy drain from the Atlantic states in moving the crops, combined to break the strongest institution on the Pacific coast.

Ralston, the plunger and promoter, had far overreached himself.

The Bonanza Kings knew of the bank's embarrassments some time in advance of its closing, for the officials had offered Flood and his firm control if they would protect the depositers.

"They offered us one million security against loss, but what is one million against a probable loss of thirteen million," said James Flood in declining. However, there was more behind his refusal than an apparent gamble.

Thirteen million in deposits and nine million in overdrafts was the bank's statement. Although $200,000 of Flood's money was on deposit, and $17,000 of the Con Virginia's owners, the financier of the Big Bonanza made no move to withdraw these amounts from the bank.

William Sharon was beaten, but not out of the race. Once

again that amazing executive ability and daring persistency of purpose came to the fore. He addressed the huge crowd pressing against the closed doors of the bank. Pale and nervous, he promised them that it would reopen on September 15. This was an embarrassment, but not a calamity, he maintained.

He then turned to the group of directors huddled in their inner sanctum. Delay would mean death to the firm, he informed them. Already the San Francisco stock exchange was threatening to close. The panic must be checked, or the Comstock would be paralyzed. His speech was well calculated to bring about his wishes. He offered one million dollars of his own to save the institution. There was but one course for the others to follow. D. O. Mills, Michael Reese, and J. R. Keene each subscribed the same amount. With another million from interested parties, a total of five million was turned over to the bank.

Ralston had been excluded from this meeting, held Friday, August 27, 1875. When he was asked to appear, the great syndicate demanded his resignation from the managerial office. It was a broken man who pleaded to remain, swearing that he would pay dollar for dollar to the depositors, and fifty cents on the dollar to the stockholders. The excited discussion which followed terminated in his defeat. He turned over all his property to Sharon for the benefit of the creditors. His death by drowning occurred that day.

The early guardian of California industries, the Bank of California, through unwise loans and unprofitable investments, had relinquished the right to the scepter of financial authority in the West. Perhaps it was just as well, since its initial purpose of giving lifeblood toward the development of the state had changed to the obverse. For some years now, the struggling frontier had been feeding the mammoth monopoly.

8

In less than six weeks the Bank of California reopened. Deposits exceeded withdrawals by thousands of dollars, since confidence had been restored in the public mind. But this institution would not regain its place in the sun. A new bank in San Francisco—the Nevada—had carefully arranged its piles of coin on the trays and stood ready for business a few days after the reopening of the old. Five hundred thousand dollars in deposits passed across its walnut counters the first day.

No wonder the Bonanza Kings had not been interested in taking over the floundering Bank of California. As early as May 25, they had incorporated their bank, but no single building available was large enough for its needs. Therefore they bought the many structures of the Nevada Block at Pine and Montgomery Streets, in San Francisco, and cleared the space for a new $1,200,00 edifice.

The real vaults of the Nevada Bank were the great bonanza in the depths of Mount Davidson. Of its five stockholders—Mackay, Fair, Vice-President Flood, and O'Brien—each owned 23,750 shares, valued at $2,375,000. President Louis McLane, an original incorporator of the rival bank, had 5000 shares worth $500,000. A flattering array of moneyed names it was, but would they be sufficient to deflect the poisoned shafts of adversity that would surely come in the future?

Fair's statement, "The Bank was the outgrowth of *my* mining enterprises," was not heard by the lode, intent upon a real Comstock celebration following the resumption of business by the Bank of California. The inhabitants remembered that it was money advanced by this bank which had developed the early Belcher and Crown Point bonanzas.

Virginia City satisfied itself with a mass meeting on the corner of C and Taylor Streets, enlivened by the Washington Guard brass band, a few bonfires, and a half-dozen salutes. Not so, Gold Hill. A torchlight procession, the participants carrying transparencies reading: "Ralston's Monument—the Afraid?" "Hail to the Chief—Uncle Billy Sharon," etc., marched to the residences of Hank Donnelly and W. P. Bennett of the Belcher mine, the Gold Hill brass band playing a few numbers, then continued to the Bank of California. A funeral dirge completed this part of the program.

Mackay and Fair were sitting comfortably in the former's home, enjoying a glass of wine from the large store in the basement. Bonfires were blazing on the surrounding hills, salutes were being fired at Fort Homestead and on Imperial Hill. The final salute at the Imperial mine caused such a concussion that Mackay and Fair were fairly jolted from their chairs. Roofs and walls of a dozen cottages were partially blown off, windows broken, furniture upset, transoms smashed in many business houses, and residences forced three inches off their foundations.

"Do you remember four-five years ago," Mackay asked his partner, "when Gold Hill 'stood in' on the occasion of some celebration or other?"

"The Fourth of July," supplemented James Fair. "Gold Hill was nearly blown into the Carson Sink that time."

"Nearly half the town was burnt down before the night was over," Mackay continued, recalling how the town marshal had climbed Imperial Hill just in time to prevent the setting off of an enormous amount of explosives.

Crazy little village of Gold Hill! It held a warm place in John Mackay's affection though, for here lay the buried glory of the great Kentuck mine.

9

Dan De Quille, "urbane Knight of the Quill," as he was called, returned to the Comstock two weeks after the recovery of the Bank of California. He was amazed to find a prosperous and flourishing pair of cities on the desert. Immediately he sought out the man he respected and admired most of all, John Mackay.

He informed him that his book on the history of the Big Bonanza was completed, most of it having been written while he was residing with Mark Twain in the East. In a few months the publishers were to send him a sample copy, Dan De Quille further stated, at which date he intended to quit newspaper work and devote his time to canvassing for subscribers. The Nevada agency had been reserved for him.

"Dan, if you keep straight with respect to drink, and bring your book out, I'll take five hundred to a thousand copies of it," Mackay promised him.[6]

With the best intentions in the world, the reporter gathered over a thousand names of subscribers among the best men of Washoe; then, unable to resist the craving for liquor, he went on a spree. The next time John Mackay saw him, he was in the county hospital, his long, frail body in a shattered condition, his collections gone.

Though Dan De Quille lost the huge bonus for abstinence, this authentic historian of the lode remained a friend of millionaire Mackay. "To John Mackay, Esq., Prince of Miners and 'Boss of the Big Bonanza,' is this book respectfully inscribed." Thus he had dedicated his story of the great lead.

7   "Sand" of Flesh and Blood

1

It was the twenty-fifth of October, 1875. Father Manogue, future bishop of Sacramento, present friend and advisor of the miners, stood before the organ in St. Mary's Cathedral working on an important problem. Could the bellows, now so laboriously supplied with air by hand, be worked by some other power? Water power perhaps? Water, the curse of the Comstock! Too much water on the Con Virginia's 1,400-foot level, John Mackay had told him. Too much water in all the mines. Too little water, with no pressure, for the increased population of the lode. The demand had already far exceeded the supply.

At six o'clock on the following morning, James Fair was at the great mines, his thoughts straying back to the fine reception he had given General Sheridan on the twentieth. John Mackay was looking, not at the past, but at the future as he prepared to make his descent into the Con Virginia. He was thinking of the Virginia City agency for the Nevada Bank, to be opened sometime in December on the corner of C and Taylor Streets opposite the Bank of California branch.

At this moment the quavering lips of the lode cried out the one word that Mackay had feared for many years. FIRE! The clanging of bells and the mourn of steam whistles brought the sleepy village to its feet.

Having started from an overturned lamp in Crazy Kate Shay's lodginghouse on A Street, the flames spread quickly to Stewart Street, igniting one house after another in their sweep toward E and G Streets. On to the business district the sparks traveled, igniting the courthouse, the building of the Washoe Club, the International Hotel, John Jack's Theatre, and Piper's Opera House. These in turn vomited flames to the Methodist, Episcopal, and Catholic churches. Like burning ships they soon reared their blazing spires from an ocean of fire below.

Washoe zephyrs from the west whipped the mounting flames into a gale of fury. Wet blankets and buckets of water were futile; the fire leapt over the fighting men and women. With insufficient water pressure, the hand engines of the fire company were useless. The feeble stream from the hose became a fine mist that disappeared before it could strike the ground. Working from a flaming half-mile square, the tenuous columns of heat traveled down the slopes of Virginia, picking up the flimsy makeshift dwellings and carrying their burning cotton partitions to other housetops.

The population was forced to recede before this bombardment of fiery cinders. Firemen pounded on doors and shouted to awaken the sleeping; glass exploded on every side and walls toppled in a shower of clapping bricks. On, on, the gray waves crawled, sending out red arrows of destruction that licked at the few possessions clutched in panic-stricken arms.

People in Carson City, sixteen miles away, could see the flames rise and fall as the furnace of heat increased in fury or burned itself out. The entire business district had to be abandoned. John Mackay knew that his house on the corner of Howard and Taylor was in the path of the white heat, but his thoughts were not on these possessions. It was the mines that must be protected at any cost. The hungry wind, in defiance of the Giant powder that razed one building after another, carried the flames toward the valuable hoisting works of the great Con Virginia. Every man to the mines! This was the last stand!

The thousands of feet of dry cordwood, stored for winter outside the Bonanza mines, began to smoke. Millions of feet of timber (for tunnel supports) flared like cellophane. The Con Virginia alone provided a bonfire of 800 cords of wood, and 1,250,000 feet of lumber. As the passenger and freight depots of the Virginia & Truckee Railroad became engulfed in flames, Mackay abandoned his work of dynamiting houses adjoining the hoisting works, since the two large buildings themselves were doomed. The fire had glided to them along the ground, and there was but one thing to do—close the Con Virginia mine.

First the men must be removed from the deep levels. There must be no rush for the hoist, no crowding, no panic.

Order and discipline alone would save them all. The time-keeper was instructed to call the workers as usual. Mackay stationed a guard of men, armed with pick handles, about the shaft opening to prevent the emerging men from running wildly into the flames. To the surface glided one load after another, each man's name being called and checked from the list of those at work. About them, the hoisting building was wrapped in fire.

The engineer stood at his post, keeping the engine going, though the flames licked greedily at him. With his thoughts only on the safety of the others, he did not realize that he was receiving severe burns. Wet blankets for him! went the order. These had to be changed in a few moments.

"That is all!" cried the timekeeper at last, and John Mackay breathed a silent prayer of thankfulness. By the time the last man stepped from the hoist, two-thirds of the building around it was gone.

Now came the most important part—the clearing of the mine. The shaft must be closed completely because, if fire descended into the underground forest, the California, Ophir, Mexican, Union Con, and Sierra Nevada mines, connected with the Con Virginia, would suck the flames into their workings from the passages below. That would mean the entire north portion of the lode was finished. Possessing the wealth of the world, Virginia could become another ghost town, haunted by the thousands who had labored so faithfully to develop it.

John Mackay had prepared for just such an emergency as this. Some time previously he had insisted upon a special precaution at the great shaft. Twenty feet below the surface he had had iron doors placed, which could be shut by pulling a ring; and above, another trap to pull up, which allowed a layer of sand twelve feet deep to pour in, the two thus forming a bulkhead. With all the men out of the mine, these things were done and the shaft closed.

Along with the hoisting works of the Con Virginia, its ore house burned, and the battery department, mill, and hoisting works of the California mine. Books and records were fortunately saved from both. Through herculean efforts the new C. & C. shaft, the most costly on the lode, was preserved.

John Mackay felt a horrible nausea from the fumes of mercury in the air. Several tons of quicksilver from the mill were smouldering, making the strongest men falter. Mackay's mind worked like a reflex as he directed the dynamiting of all houses adjoining the California stamp mill and the new pan mill. Fair was there, giving orders which were followed with military precision; discipline and system had always been his policy as superintendent.

The shadows were lengthening by the time success was insured for the Bonanza mines. At this moment Mackay saw a man trying to start a fire in one of the buildings. No sooner was this new menace taken care of than Sam Curtis, superintendent of the Ophir, rushed to Mackay to say that the fire from that mine's hoisting works had set fire to its shaft. The heat was so intense that the wheels of the cars of the railroad directly opposite had been melted. Water thrown down the smoking aperture of the Ophir was ineffectual. Mackay realized that the flames might work further into the mine and communicate with the connecting California level. He ordered several men to place a hand engine near the Con Virginia mill's reservoir. The powerful stream thus furnished soon extinguished the shaft fire.

It was 6:00 P.M. Two thousand buildings had been leveled to the ground in twelve hours. Ten million dollars in property were in reeking ashes. Eight thousand homeless persons huddled about a few belongings on bleak Mount Davidson, trying to smile as the children complained of their hard beds. Remarkable was the fact that only two persons were fatally burned, and a very few others injured from falling walls and minor burns.

The "Boys in Blue" had arrived, and they began enforcing martial law and prohibiting the remaining saloons from selling liquor. Carson City sent bread, blankets, and mattresses. Private homes, in addition to the restaurants and bakeries of the capital, were cooking to full capacity. Special trains carried these provisions to the hungry population of the lode. Farmers in California and Nevada furnished tons of produce, while the cities dispatched coin subscriptions, fuel, and clothing to the devastated area.

All of the Comstock neighbors offered accommodations.

2

At the height of the conflagration, an Irishwoman had rushed to Mackay, screaming, "The church—the church—is on fire!"

"Damn the church!" Mackay had answered with impatience. "If we can keep the fire out of the shafts, we can build another!"

In 1876 a new edifice, larger, more durable and beautiful, was to stand on the black ruins of the old church, the gift of John Mackay and his wife. When the buildings of the Con Virginia and California were no more, St. Mary's in the Mountains would be intact, a monument to a once great city of twenty thousand persons.

More than the church or the mines interested Mackay the morning after the fire. It was the pitiful condition of hundreds of families that received his foremost attention.

"There is a good deal of suffering here, Father," he told the priest, who was surprised at the miner's early visit. "If I try to help personally I shall be caught by two or three grafters and then will be liable to insult some worthy men and women. I turn the business over to you and your lieutenants. Do it thoroughly, and when you need help draw upon me and keep drawing."[1]

Father Manogue not only understood miners but millionaire John Mackay. In the next ninety days $150,000 were withdrawn from Mackay's personal account. Meanwhile, Mackay himself was busy replacing the costly machinery and the buildings which had been destroyed.

The Bonanza mines took the lead in helping the lode toward recovery. While the Con Virginia lumber yards were still a mass of smoking embers, Mackay and Fair set men to work clearing and preparing the ground for the new hoisting works. There was much to be salvaged—despoiled machinery, great amounts of quicksilver, $90,000 worth of bullion. Mackay had already ordered several carloads of timber from the firm's fluming business in Washoe County. Sharon had promised him that the railroad would be repaired immediately to permit the lumber to be shipped right to the mine.

"In a few months the ore will be coming to the surface in the new hoisting works," Mackay told reporters. "The Con Virginia mill, however, won't be rebuilt until spring, as we can't get the necessary machinery."

He was occupied for many days letting contracts for new portions of machinery, a new air compressor, and ordering a thousand things. About him swarmed hundreds of workmen receiving supplies, replacing, repairing. Carpenters were putting together the gallows frame for the Con Virginia shaft; stonemasons and bricklayers were preparing the foundation for the machinery; engineers were testing the boilers; unskilled laborers were stacking the shipments of timber that arrived daily; machinists, millwrights, and foundrymen were moving about in a workshop where everything, including the new dump, was to be larger and better than before.

James Fair directed activities underground, developing the unproductive Gould & Curry on its 1,700-foot level and using its shaft to hoist some of the Con Virginia ore. Day and night the work went on, since the Bonanza mines had to bolster the stock market, greatly weakened by the closing of the Ophir shaft and the uselessness of the Con Virginia shaft.

The loss to the Bonanza mines totaled almost a million and a half dollars, but the kings vowed that dividends should not cease at a time when the lode needed them most. In November and December Mackay announced a dividend of $10 a share, which totaled $1,080,000 for the stockholders. In addition, the expanded pay roll helped hundreds of men formerly employed in other branches of work.

Heavy rains, snow, and a tornado hindered building, but no one dared to lose heart. How to keep the seven mills working—those formerly run on Con Virginia ore, was Mackay's immediate problem. Tailings was the solution, he decided. So tailings it was that kept the millmen of the Bacon, Trench, Woodworth, Morgan, Brunswick, Occidental, and Mariposa mills busy.

Up to the day of the fire, the old Gould & Curry whistle, most remarkable in sound, had regulated the time in Virginia City. But on November 15, blown by mistake one hour too early—4:40 A.M.—it fell into disrepute. Henceforth, the four new whistles that Mackay had had installed at the completed Con Virginia hoisting works, became the official timekeepers of the Comstock. Their reliability was soon undisputed.

Just one and a half months after the fire, rich ore again rose through the great mine's shaft. In another week, the mine was "going full blast," according to Mackay, producing six hundred tons a day. The stock market began to recover. Mackay announced that during the coming year production of this mine would probably surpass that of 1875 due to improved facilities for hoisting and crushing.

Fair was driving the C. & C. shaft along at an unprecedented speed. By the close of the year the great aperture was down 1,020 feet.

3

There were the usual rumors to deny. This time the story circulated that Sharon was through, that his Ophir mine had passed into the hands of the Bonanza Kings.

"The California mine is merely using the Ophir shaft for hoisting some of its ore," Mackay vigorously denied.

Sharon had lost prestige but, though silenced, he was not impotent.

Mackay's trips to San Francisco were necessarily infrequent because Virginia had requisitioned all her citizens to banish the spectacle of desolation. He was on a Committee of Ten to decide how the streets might be widened, and to consider means of increasing the water supply. No repetition of the last horror must ever occur. There should be at least water for such emergencies. The demand for water had increased rapidly, far beyond the supply available and far beyond the expectations of the Virginia and Gold Hill Water Company.

The firm promptly extended its flume eight and a half miles farther to Marlette Lake, which had a storage capacity of over two billion gallons. Then a second pipe line was laid alongside the first, doubling the amount of water available to the Comstock. In order to increase the pressure, tanks were constructed on the hills above the city, with pipes extending to the town. Hydrants were placed at adequate intervals on the streets.

Captain J. B. Overton, superintendent of the company, designed and laid this second pipe, as well as a third line later. From Marlette Lake the water traveled north through a covered flume for five miles, east through a four-thousand-foot tunnel dug through a dividing ridge that formed the eastern rim of the Lake Tahoe basin, then south six and a half miles to join the pipe lines crossing Washoe Valley.

Several reservoirs were built which held from 3,000,000 to 10,000,000 gallons, and the water company announced that it could supply over 7,000,000 gallons of water every twenty-four hours.

Sam Davis, historian of Nevada, claimed that the total water works cost the enterprising firm $3,500,000.

It was well that John Mackay had grown in mining stature, because there were future dragons to slay. For one who loved more and hated less than he would admit, even to himself, there were to be many disheartening moments of defeat.

8 An Artificial Big Bonanza

1

Marie-Louise Mackay came to Virginia at the end of March, 1876, for a brief visit. Though the newly rebuilt town had improved in appearance, she observed that cows, hogs, and goats were still roaming the streets.

James Fair was in Washington, D.C., so Mackay had little time to devote to his wife. Production of the Con Virginia had increased from six hundred to nine hundred tons of ore a day, and a new winze below the 1,500-foot level of the California mine showed the gangue of the vein to be covered with globules and spangles of pure silver.

With little here to interest Mrs. Mackay, she returned to San Francisco. Two weeks passed, and still her husband did not find time to go "below." Fair would not be back until the twenty-first of April, Mackay telegraphed her, so he had much to prepare for the Bonanza exhibit at the Philadelphia exposition.

This was the Centennial year. Each of four cars was to take eleven tons of ore for crushing in mills erected on the fair grounds. Average ore must be sacked and choice specimens labeled, to provide the greatest display of wealth ever to be shown to the American public. He could not leave now.

Thus Mrs. Mackay returned to the lode in order to complete plans for a trip to Europe. This time she intended to make her home on the Continent until the children's formal education was completed. John Mackay promised to accompany the family if they would stop for a few days at the fair before continuing to Paris.

He needed rest and solitude after the troubles of the past year. The accusations of his firm's enemies when the Bank of

California failed, the horror of the great fire, and the strain resulting from the rush in the mines, might be erased by this vacation. He therefore refused the appointment of judge of minerals at the Centennial since this trip already had enough snags and sawyers. Eventually he must make a choice between his two loves—his family, or this enigmatic and uncertain realm.

2

Meanwhile the West was wondering how the wealth of the Bonanza Kings would change its owners. Would it reduce the stature of others as it enlarged their own range of vision?

A San Francisco stock report of March 23, 1876, states:

Mr. Fair informed us the other day while on the subject of the marvelous appreciation of the Con Virginia, and the immense fortunes accumulated by early holders of its stocks, that they had started in with some $40,000 in the early part of the decade. The amount of their wealth cannot at present be computed, even by themselves. Fair said it might be set down in round figures at eighty million, though that sum would not begin to buy out their various interests.

How will the possession of all this boundless, unestimable wealth affect the very fortunate quartet? Will the power which monied wealth brings, make them forget the common amenities of life and what they owe to their fellow citizens? Will they exercise the power which the Goddess of Fortune has endowed them with to avoid carrying their share of the public burden; or will their souls expand with their increase of wealth and consequent ability, and induce them to shoulder a still greater and more proportionate share of the burden? Two of these four have sought for and earned their great wealth by patient toil, unremitting exertion and rewarding success in years of underground exploration. The other two have been made rich by their connection with the first mentioned. All four are now rich beyond their wildest anticipations . . . and it remains to be seen what good or bad use they will make of their present wealth and power.

The average estimate of their fortune was around $100,-000,000. It was a common remark that Mackay's income was $800,000 a month. When the coming July would put the California mine on the dividend-paying list, with a monthly payment of $150,000 to the stockholders, Mackay would average a million a month. So figured the world. It had forgotten that he had been near ruin twice, and in those days of surprise and constant change, he might become a pauper in a few days.

There was one other thing that the imaginative Pacific coast forgot—the ever-present, insoluble struggle with nature. Already a rumble was heard in the mountain cleft. May dividends of the two great mines dropped to two dollars each, resulting in a decline of the stock market.

Colonel Fair remained imperturbable. Even Mackay, escorting ex-Governor Pacheco of California through the "internal revenue arrangements" of the Bonanza mines, was startled by Fair's bland remark, "When the new 80-stamp mill of the Con Virginia is completed, I expect to be turning out five million in bullion a month. It is only a question of mining facilities, and not a lack of ore."

Mackay hurried his guest into the cage, and was silent.

3

Senator Sharon had bowed to the new satrap of the Comstock by having his private "palace" car renovated for the use of John Mackay and family on their trip east. The week of May 21 witnessed their sumptuous arrival in the Centennial city.

To Mackay, of eager ear but unwilling mouth, the interminable flow of questions that followed him in Philadelphia was very tiring. He could not be genial or ever confidential in manner to strangers. His early reserve, developed recently into a marked constraint, due to a desire not to be misunderstood, was absent only in the presence of friends. Taciturn and isolated in a crowd, he needed the courtly ease of James Fair, whose ready chuckles, lack of ceremony, and amazing tolerance, rendered him capable of jesting with stranger and friend alike. Mackay the millionaire, like John the miner of Mex, was no actor.

Nob Hill in San Francisco had turned a starched face from Mrs. Mackay, but the magnificent residence that her husband leased for her upon arriving in Paris was calculated to impress the French. It was an interested American colony, too, that watched her initial steps at establishment at the head of the avenue des Champs Elysées, close to the Arc de Triomphe, in what they considered a large hotel.

According to the stories circulated, Mr. Mackay agreed to help her furnish it in a fitting manner. Toward this end he engaged an American whose responsibility was to purchase the furniture, drapes, etc. Due to the fact that neither the family nor the merchant knew anything about furnishing a house in "the French manner," the result was said to be amazing. Paris was dumbfounded at the extravagant waste of money, "with no taste, or at least with bad taste."[1]

Wrote the Paris correspondent for the *San Francisco Chronicle*:

Just here appears a certain Count, an elderly gentleman of expensive tastes which, during a long lifetime, he has gratified at the cost of other people.

His setting sun is declining upon a life well spent in fleecing not only his own countrymen but rich foreigners, who need the assistance of a man of refined tastes to help them live in this great city, and to do what many foolish Americans here wish to do—get into French society (about as profligate, licentious, and false as any society can be and not fall to pieces from inherent rottenness).

The Count managed to have Mr. Mackay brought to him and introduced into his house. In return for this condescension, he invited the Count to the Mackay mansion.

Mr. and Mrs. Mackay asked him how he liked the way their house was furnished. [He] told them it was not at all French and that if they expected to enter Paris society, they must change all. Thereupon Mr. Mackay and his wife begged the Count to do it over in true Parisian taste.

Of course it would not have looked well for the Count to go about spending the Mackays' money for them, and acting as an humble commission merchant. He suggested to Mackay the appointment of a certain Frenchman as private secretary, steward, chamberlain, etc. This man was appointed. Through him, all the purchases for a complete refurnishing were made, the other furniture being shipped off to the States for Mr. Mackay's American home.

Thus the rule was made that every purchase, down to the smallest item for Mrs. Mackay's establishment, had to be authorized by the chamberlain, the Count receiving a liberal percentage for each addition to the elaborate household.

"The largest art-publishing firm in the world told an artist friend," the reporter further related, "that he had repeatedly tried to sell Mrs. Mackay paintings, and has never yet succeeded because his house will not pay the Count the extravagant commission he demands."

It was an unnatural John Mackay who attempted to mix easy amiabilities with the strangers swarming through his mansion. Made ill at ease by the cajolery of countless women, finding it difficult to judge this new world that turned on a trifle solely by its conversation instead of its intentions, he realized that he could never be completely happy away from the mines.

Yet he wanted Mrs. Mackay to shine in all the glorious display that he scorned for himself. He would do all in his power to help her scale the heights of her social ambition, encouraging her to spend more than a queen if it would make her happy.

The "Rocket of the Comstock" knew his guilelessness and immense wealth made him hunted prey for the sycophants of Europe. He was far too unpretentious for the Parisian society of 1876.

4

Back to the States he sailed, recalling how lovely Indian summer was on the lode, knowing that the world of activity awaiting him was not synthetic and that the withered old desert was far kinder than the frivolous cities which boasted eternal youth. Every mine was different and every day promised the unexpected. Therein lay the challenge to a master. Had Mackay been nothing more than an ordinary laborer in the mines, his love of the Comstock would have been as deeply ingrained.

On August 11, he left the railroad at Reno to complete the trip to Virginia City by carriage. There were hundreds of letters waiting for him—mostly from persons wanting money. A woman in Washington wrote that her daughter had been slandered. Would he kindly forward fifteen hundred dollars with which to hire counsel?

Colonel Fair had had his troubles during his partner's absence. July 12, the "bears" had started the report that Mackay had gone insane in Europe. A week later, James Flood paid one of his extremely rare visits to the mines, thereby causing numerous dispatches to be sent to San Francisco announcing the "petering out" of the Bonanza mines. With Mackay's return to the coast, Flood felt free to make his long-planned trip to New York City. San Francisco put its many heads together and whispered that the Bonanza firm was going to establish a branch of the Nevada Bank in the East.

For lack of any other member of the quartet, plump and genial O'Brien was consulted for verification of the rumor.

"All our interests are this side of the slope. We would no more send bullion to New York than to a foreign country," he remarked over a hand of "cinch"—A California form of "seven-up." O'Brien's statement would not be true for long.

This jolly bachelor, of widely spaced eyes and full jowls flanking a goatee, was content to be the ornamental member of the clan. He had no greater ambitions than to continue drawing his monthly dividend of three hundred thousand dollars. Devoted to fine horses, he could be seen frequently after five o'clock riding his trick white Arabian, or driving his sleek Hambletonian trotters to the Cliff House. This was the popular daily rendezvous for San Francisco businessmen.

5

The mines of the Comstock were besieged with visitors, who required no little attention and watching. Though few could recognize ore when they saw it, the shareholders considered it their duty, in the face of new rumors of ore exhaustion, to inspect every level. Superintendent Fair didn't disappoint them as he held his lamp high to throw light on the shining surface of walls and ceiling. "Terrible rich. Terrible rich," he would murmur as if to himself, and would follow the declaration with a deep sigh of satisfaction.

There is the story of a woman who, owning a few shares of stock, insisted upon visiting the lower levels of Savage. Mackay, having completed his inspection of Hale & Norcross, entered the Savage on his way to the Gould & Curry and the Con Virginia just as the woman expressed a desire to go deeper. Mackay escorted her into the hot and foul lower galleries, whereupon she immediately became nauseated and dizzy. She demanded a quick return to the surface.

"Then you don't want to see the big V-bob?" Mackay asked her.

"I couldn't stand to see anything bob right now. I want to get out of here!" she gasped as the cage carried her upwards.

U.S. Grant, Jr., of special interest to Mackay; Senator Morton, of Indiana; Secretary of War Cameron; and grey-haired General Sherman were more distinguished visitors. What must this warrior of the Civil War have thought as "Captains" by the score attended "Colonel" Fair's luncheon in his honor!

Ostensibly all was well with the Big Bonanza; in reality, Mackay was helplessly watching the black clouds of a national panic gather over his mines. More disastrous and far-reaching than the stock market crash of a year ago was the

Old playbill at Piper's Opera House
Courtesy Museum of Memories, Virginia City, Nevada

John William Mackay
Courtesy Acme Newspictures

Mrs. John Mackay in her wedding dress, 1867
Courtesy Martin Behrman Collection

The first type of "iron horse" used on the Virginia & Truckee Railroad

Mackay's residence on the corner of
Howard and Taylor streets, Virginia City. It was burned in the great fire.
Courtesy Martin Behrman Collection

One of the earliest fire fighting units of Virginia City

A Wells Fargo Express Messenger ready for business

James Graham Fair

panic of silver! For the first time in American history, silver had dropped below par with gold!

6

In Europe, with the great men of finance, John Mackay had had opportunity to learn some of the causes for the rapid demonetization of this precious metal. It was strangely connected with the payment of the Franco-German war idemnity.

According to the Treaty of Frankfurt, signed May 10, 1871, France agreed to pay Germany, within the next three years, the sum of one billion dollars. A little over one-tenth of the amount was to be paid in specie, and the remaining portion in bills of exchange, based on French credits in other countries.

At this time France was considered the leading nation in the possession of gold. This metal had replaced silver as legal tender following the gold discoveries of 1848 in California, and those of 1851 in Australia. Between 1848 and 1860 France coined more than one hundred million pounds of gold, exporting at the same time an equal amount in silver.

But it so happened that while she was paying her war debt to Germany, more gold than was intended found its way out of the country, resulting in a loss of approximately two hundred million dollars' worth of that metal. In the meantime, France gained thirteen million in silver. Germany, on the other hand, while losing about thirteen million in silver, knew she would receive a large share of this migratory French gold, so promptly utilized this opportunity for changing from a silver to a gold currency.

Up to this time the currency of Germany had consisted of silver coins and bank notes based on silver—the largest of these coins, the thalers, being legal tender to an unlimited amount. But confusion was prevalent throughout the nation, since its thirty-odd independent states had almost as many systems of money. Even in those states where the systems were similar, the coins themselves differed considerably.

Thus the rulers of Germany, intent upon uniting the country, decided first to adopt a uniform system of money for the entire domain. All French francs being paid to the government were recoined upon receipt into marks, and Germany announced on July 9, 1873, that henceforth gold coins were the legal tender of the country.

There was one drawback, however. Only a certain amount

of gold could, practicably, be put into circulation at any one time. The silver coins had to be withdrawn gradually from use so that their sale could take place simultuneously. To facilitate this replacement of silver by gold, Germany declared that, for the time being, both old and new coins would pass as legal tender. In addition, the government fixed the weight relationship between the two metals at 15½ of silver to 1 of gold, this ratio to be maintained until such time as silver coins would no longer be considered unlimited legal tender, but their use was restricted to twenty marks in any one payment.

Meanwhile, all gold francs pouring into Germany as a portion of the war debt were sent to the mint to be coined into Imperial marks. As soon as these were placed in national circulation, the same amount of old silver coins, still of equal value to the new gold, was drawn into the mint, melted, refined, cast into bars, and offered for sale.

Onto the markets of the world began to be dumped Germany's surplus silver. With one hundred and sixty-four million dollars in silver to dispose of in the five- to six-year period set by Germany for the completion of her recoinage, there was unconsciously created in Berlin an artificial "Big Bonanza." At the very time that Belcher and Crown Point were yielding great amounts of bullion from the Comstock Lode, Germany was beginning to throw great quantities of silver on the London market. Then came the discovery of the Big Bonanza of the Comstock. Before its wealth had begun to be removed, the United States passed disastrous legislation that further hastened the panic of silver.

During the Civil War an inconvertible paper currency had been issued by the government, and with this the business of the nation was transacted; but in 1873 the United States decided to formally establish the gold dollar as the standard coin of the country. Up to this time the silver dollar of 371¼ grains fine had been at a greater premium than the gold dollar of 23.22 grains fine—the relation being considered 16 to 1. The cause for the rise in the gold value of silver was the gold discoveries of early Pacific coast history. After 1870, however, when the production of gold was dwarfed by the deluge of silver from the Western States, the price of silver, as measured with gold, began to drop, and the reverse process by which France had acquired a gold currency came into operation in the United States.

The mint stopped its coinage of the standard American silver dollar in 1873, substituting a trade dollar of 420 grains standard weight for use in the Orient to compete with the Mexican dollar. The next year the Federal statutes were further revised, a clause being inserted which limited the legal tender of silver coins to amounts not exceeding five dollars. By autumn, the silver dollar was noticeably on the downgrade, the average relation of silver to gold for the year being 16.16 to 1.

To be sure, the suspension of silver coinage in the United States alone could not have caused this fall in price. There was a mounting preference for gold throughout the world, leaving silver to find its own market. India, which had always purchased great quantities of silver, could not begin to absorb the surplus available. France, with her great loss of gold, had suspended specie payments to other nations, using her national bank notes as legal tender and permitting only small amounts of gold to circulate within her borders. The Scandinavian countries, following Germany's lead, substituted gold for silver in their monetary system, and added nine million dollars' worth of silver to the flooded market. The German mint, meanwhile, continued its sales of silver at an accelerated rate to compete with the mounting production of this metal in the United States. Three out of every five million of the Comstock's bullion was silver!

In 1875, with the annual production of the United States climbing from $25,500,000 to $30,250,000, the ratio of the silver dollar fell again, averaging 16.63 to 1 for the year. This relationship might have been maintained, with no serious effects, had not stories promulgated from the Comstock Lode itself brought about a further plunge of the white metal.

By a quirk of fate, the great lode was constantly referred to as a silver vein, and the fact that its gold portion ran from 40 to 45 per cent was only of casual interest. Thus, when Mr. H. R. Whitehill, official mineralogist of the state of Nevada, stated in his annual report of 1873-74 that there were $143,000,000 in bullion above the 1,550-foot level of the Con Virginia mine alone, Europe began to take interest. To its financiers that spelled $143,000,000 in silver!

On top of this exaggeration, Dr. Linderman, director of the United States Mint, averred that his estimate of the value of the Big Bonanza was $300,000,000. That meant to the world the same amount in *silver!* Then came the announcement of Philipp Deidesheimer, reputed to be the greatest mining engineer of the century. This expert said $1,500,000,-000! The word billion was too much for Europe. Envisioning an avalanche of silver such as it had never known sweeping onto its surfeited market, the nations began to join hands to demonetize this metal.

The Pacific coast experienced the first effects of these grossly exaggerated estimates of the wealth of the Big Bonanza—the market crash and its ruination of thousands of families. Those capitalists who made millions on the stock manipulations promptly invested the money in government bonds or outside securities. Nevada and California were both drained of much of their working capital. The failure of the powerful Bank of California was but one example of how disastrous the ensuing depression would be.

In November of 1875, Dr. Linderman issued his second report, stating that the production of the Comstock for the following year would be $50,000,000. His companian, R. E. Rogers, geologist and chemist from Pennsylvania, estimated three times this amount. The speculators of the world wanted Con Virginia and California stock. These reports took on an official mien in Germany and England when newspapers published the figures as "500,000,000 francs." The monetary affairs of the Continent went out of control. In San Francisco, Linderman's report aided the recovery of Bonanza stock. From $210 a share in October, Con Virginia stock rose to $400 in November; from $250 in September, California shares jumped to $375 in the next two months.

The Latin Union, consisting of France, Belgium, Italy, Roumania, Switzerland, and Greece, had suspended the free coinage of silver in 1874 when the demonetized silver of Germany threatened to flood their mints. On August 5, 1876, France closed her mint to silver. Eastern trade began to feel very insecure as only two countries—Germany and England—continued gold payments.

England appointed a parliamentary committee to consider the depreciation of silver; the United States appointed an American Silver Commission and began to issue countless works on the subject.

Now Mackay had occasion to regret that he had not denied the extravagant estimates than being published; that he had not checked the unwarranted publicity of the mines' magnified wealth. Though he had not affirmed the reports, rebuke was to be directed at him for not decrying his own property. Adolph Sutro had learned a few years earlier that the Franco-Prussian War was disastrous—subscriptions of funds from European capitalists for his tunnel having been canceled at its inception; but no one paid any attention to Sutro.

With the silver panic in full career, the world realized at last that its silver mints could not possibly utilize all the metal available for coinage. However, the leaders on the Comstock fissure were not to sit calmly by while more than half of its bullion remained in disrepute.

9   Evasion and Escape

1

"They are like two buckets on the end of a rope," remarked a Con Virginia miner, in referring to the alternate San Francisco trips of Mackay and Fair. "When one comes up, the other goes down."[1]

The consternation caused by the fact that both superintendents were located staying at the Palace Hotel during the same week in 1876, supported the aptness of this comparison. Reporters from the *Alta* and the *Chronicle* shadowed the pair, only to have their best suspicions confirmed—Mackay and Fair had quarreled! The cause of friction was apparently the evasion of tax payments on Bonanza ore.

In 1867 a law had been passed in Storey County, Nevada, requiring a county tax of $1.50 on every one hundred dollars' worth of property, but only twenty-five cents on the same amount of bullion from the mines. This unfair arrangement was altered later by the state bullion tax, which made mineowners—wealthiest of the citizenry—pay the same amount on ore as the miners had been doing on property, the tax amounting to ninety cents on one hundred dollars.

This was still "discrimination in favor of one class, such as is not provided for in the rules of political economy, but which had its origin in the generous spirit of the lawmakers and people. They placed a tax on a farmer's crop without any regard to his seed and labor, taxed the product of the mechanic's skill without deduction for time or cost, taxed the merchant according to his goods, and the laborer according to his wealth and possessions," yet only the *net* proceeds of the mines were required to be taxed, a large percentage being allowed for mining and milling costs."[2]

The revenue from this Bonanza tax was to furnish a great part of the running expenses of Nevada's 104,000 square miles of territory, a large area populated by only fifty thousand persons. The disastrously depleted state treasury hoped to extricate itself from difficulty by means of this splendid source of income.

A serious snag appeared when the two great companies—Con Virginia and California—took steps toward resisting payment of the tax just before the November, 1876, election. They insisted the tax was excessive and the law unconstitutional. The Bonanza firm would test the legality of this new legislation in the courts!

Fair's contention was that Sharon had harvested his mines on the low rating, but now, with the Bonanza mines at the height of production—from 675 to 1000 tons a day—Sharon was the loudest in maintaining that the tax was just.

"Just," Fair said sarcastically, "because the interest on the bonds issued by Ormsby and Storey counties for the construction of Sharon's railroad is long overdue."

The two political parties vied with each other in promising the greatest relief to the people, and in exacting the most binding pledges from the candidates. But the election was a blow to the Bonanza Kings. Not a man under their influence achieved office. An added annoyance was the seizure of a large amount of Bonanza bullion by the assessor of Storey County for overdue taxes. By the close of 1876, the California Mining Company owed $60,571.40 and the Con Virginia Company, $51,806.31. Mackay and Fair had to give an oath that the real estate of the mines was sufficient security for the debt before the assessor would release the bullion.

2

When the legislature convened the first of the year, 1877, Colonel Fair engaged rooms over the Carson City Savings Bank and began to campaign for the passage of a new bill —the Bullion Tax Compromise Bill. He buttonholed all the prominent men in Carson, treated them to champagne and cigars, counseled with the lobby, and ingratiated himself with the reporters. There was a hint of money exchanging hands. John Mackay remained aloof, trying to reconcile himself to the actual posture of affairs. Fair could not be "bossed."

The proposed law was sent to the Senate for consideration. As it stood, it attempted to exempt 60 per cent of all ores milling less than $100 a ton, and 50 per cent of the value of ores milling more than $100 a ton. This would grant immunity to fully one-half of the proceeds subject to taxation.

Fair, as the mouthpiece of the Bonanza firm, urged the support of the compromise bill on the promise that, if passed, the two mines would pay the delinquent taxes, thereby reducing the rate of taxation on real and personal property to seventy-five cents on $100. But if the tax on the mines was to be reduced from 20 per cent to 50 per cent of their net proceeds, then the rate on other property must be correspondingly enlarged in order that the state might derive the same amount of income. How much easier it would be to reduce taxes by requiring the mining property to bear its share of the burden, instead of releasing it from taxes.

The judiciary committee was of this opinion, and its members declared the proposed compromise to be directly opposed to the constitution, an unjust discrimination in favor of the mining corporations and owners, and an unwarranted oppression on all other classes of property and industry. In spite of its attitude, the Senate passed the bill 14 to 11.

Earnestly the Bonanza Kings labored for its support in the House. Petitions were circulated to release members from their pledges, galleries of the capital were jammed with anxious men attempting to show the value of every amendment. Once again money was supreme. The bill passed the House 27 to 23. Governor Bradley, honest "Old Broadhorns," received it next, and defeated it with his veto. As the legislature adjourned, Mackay and Fair tried a new strategy.

In an attempt to gain a stay of execution of the tax enforcement, the two mineowners signed bonds of $120,000 for each of the mining companies involved. This denied, their fructuous imagination suggested another compromise. They offered to Storey County $80,000 for the school, general, and sinking funds, but not one dollar of it for railroad bonds. This sum was to be an advance until the lawsuits with the state were settled. It was not a loan or a payment on delinquent taxes. However, if the Bonanza firm lost the fight, then the $80,000 must be deducted from the amount of the judgment against them. In the event that the kings won in court, Storey County and not the state might keep the sum as a gift.

It would appear that the idea was to conciliate the people of the county where taxes were paid and where Mackay and Fair resided, permitting only this portion of the state to be relieved of money worries in case of their defeat. As a further inducement, they promised to advance quarterly a sum equal to one-half of 1 per cent of the net bullion product of the two mines for community use.

Excluding other portions of the state from a share in this revenue, portions where incomes were very small, was the very thing Governor Bradley was fighting. What would Storey County decide? If it did not accept the $80,000 immediately, it would be necessary to levy in April a $1.50 tax on every one hundred dollars' worth of property in the county for general purposes, and a fifty-cent tax for school funds.

The *San Francisco Chronicle* explained:

Besides the humiliation which the acceptance of this proposed bribe would entail upon the Commissioners, and through them upon the county, there are objections to its acceptance based on purely legal principles, which it may be well to consider. The theory is, that this money which is now offered to the county, is not a payment of taxes due, but an advance generously tendered by Mackay and Fair. It is not a loan, for the county pays no interest for its use, gives no security for its repayment, does not in fact even agree to refund it to the Bonanza men. It is not a gift. . . . The result of its acceptance is the State will step in and claim her share of the spoils, some 90% of the gross amount. If the Commissioners refuse to pass it over, legal proceedings will follow, and ultimately the money will have to be paid, with a large bill of costs added. Where then is Storey County the gainer by accepting this 'generous' offer? Will it not be far better for her to stand upon her dignity in this matter and say to these men, "This money which you offer us in the guise of charity, is not yours to give. It belongs to us, and we will not accept as an accommodation what is our own of right. Keep your bribe, gentlemen, and we will keep our honor and our dignity."

The plans of the Bonanza millionaires failed to materialize under the pressure of public opinion on the lode. The claims in court were just, the public maintained, so the compromise was refused. Still the controversy continued for several months longer, the attorneys in charge of the suits in Storey County finally succeeding in forcing the two mining companies to pay deliquent taxes of some $300,000 on the promise of a two-year stay of execution on the $100,000 penalty previously demanded for nonpayment of the tax. This time there was no discrimination against the railroad bonds.

3

As Mackay continued his quarrels with Fair, rumor promised that the two men were dissolving partnership, and that Sharon, Keene, and Mackay would form a new coalition. Mackay had not been so bitter as the others against the ex-king, and "Uncle Billy" had made many overtures to the new Boss of the Comstock. When reporters questioned Mackay, he pulled his busy and dramatic eyebrows together and denied the story most vehemently.

This exasperating man disliked nothing more than talking about himself or his affairs. With a sincere passion for truth, he hated improvisation, and the truth was no one's business. He also abhorred working alone, so when partnerships fit tightly, he was tolerant of censure as well as glory. Now he was forced to dam up the fount of personal feeling.

His chief diversion, the theater—the world of make-believe—offered him relaxation. Christmas Day and the succeeding four days were spent in the bay region, but "the Chief" hastened back to the lode for New Year's Eve, 1876. Lawrence Barrett was beginning an engagement at Piper's Opera House, playing the title roles in *Richelieu, Harebell,* and *Damon and Pythias.*

A few months before this, Edwin Adams, actor, had arrived in San Francisco following a badly managed and unsuccessful season in Australia. His engagement there had been poorly timed, and, to make matters ruinous, poor health had caused him to be frequently absent from the footlights.

Back in San Francisco, scene of former triumphs as the impersonator of Enoch Arden, Adams felt certain of a welcome. He and his devoted wife entered the city secretly, for his depleted funds permitted only the poorest of lodgings. Though broken in health, he began his search for employment. There were no roles for Ned Adams to play; there were no old stage friends who offered to help him. Proud and sensitive, he did not consider appealing to former associates or patrons of the theater for charity.

Week after week he made the rounds of the playhouses, his desperation mounting from continued refusals of work. How often he must have thought of the old days when he had given assistance to countless destitute actors. Suicide would have been a feeble gesture. He had nothing to bequeath to the woman who had shared his prosperity and vicissitudes with equal cheerfulness. Somehow he must manage to live and make her happy.

The days led into the chill fogs of December, and by this time Ned Adams was desperate. One afternoon his footsteps dragged more than usual as he made his way back to his miserable rooms. He did not see the Christmas shoppers burdened with gaily wrapped bundles; he dared not look into the festooned windows of the bakeries where rich fruit cakes and sugared rolls formed enticing displays.

Reaching home, his wife handed him a letter. His trembling fingers managed to tear open the envelope. Then his hopeless eyes filled with tears as the words took on meaning.

> VIRGINIA CITY, NEVADA
> Dec. 21
>
> MY DEAR MR. ADAMS,
>
> Knowing you to be in some slight financial strait, may I beg your acceptance of the inclosed accommodation and thus permit me to discharge in part the vast obligation I feel, in common with thousands of others, for your efforts in our behalf?
>
> I trust that our city may long be honored by your presence among us, and that our stage may not soon be deprived of one of its brightest ornaments.
>
> With my very best regards for your future success, and thanks for past favors, I have the honor to remain
>
> Your obliged and obedient servant,
>
> JOHN W. MACKAY.[3]

The "inclosed accommodation" was for two thousand dollars. To be sure, he could afford it, as the November cleanup of the Con Virginia alone was $1,202,236.40 for its stockholders—Mackay being the largest owner of shares.

In the months following, work in the theater became more frequent for Adams. The inked pages that had surrounded the miraculous check became worn and soiled from frequent handling. When the actor died a couple of years later, that letter was found beneath his pillow.

John McCullough, informing Mackay how greatly Adams had worshipped him, heard only a tight-lipped, "Poor fellow. I wish to God I had sent him ten thousand dollars."

4

In June of 1867, when John McCullough first performed in Virginia City, Mackay was attracted to this Irishman. He had come to San Francisco the year before to form a partnership with his distinguished contemporary, Lawrence Barrett, and for eight succeeding seasons was acclaimed the outstanding player on the Western stage, making occasional appearances in Virginia City. In the fall of 1874, upon his return from a New York engagement, McCullough was given a four-weeks' contract at $36,000!

He and Mackay were climbing at the same time. Their friendship was no accident. Separated by an apparently insuperable hedge of occupation, the two men had similar backgrounds, analagous characteristics (such as great mental as well as physical power), and an intense love of the drama. Though months often passed between their meetings, the mineowner always stopped at McCullough's rooms in the Brooklyn Hotel in San Francisco whenever the actor was on the coast.

"I never had a desire to be *called* a great actor," McCullough once said to John Mackay. "I meant to *be* a great actor."

Corresponding aims were those of a Downieville placer miner—aims made into actualities by an unrelenting observation of details and a home course of study; both men were prepared for any opportunity within their field. As blunt and direct as his friend, McCullough had none of the fiery temper of Mackay. His kind, openhearted attitude and protective calmness appealed strongly to the master miner.

While John McCullough was raising the drama to its "Golden Age" on the Pacific coast, John Mackay was opening the Big Bonanza, chief contribution to the "Silver Age" in mining history. So far, neither had been destroyed by a success trumpeted around the world. Their antitoxins for acclaim were humility and a marked contempt for the outward display of accompanying wealth, but being sincere performers, they sought admiration and praise.

Yet when tributes came to Mackay, he was unhappy if he found himself in the presence of flatterers. While eager for power, he scorned pickthanks, not so much from a dislike of those tendering homage but from an inner limitation, an unconscious feeling of inferiority that made him miserable in the thought that people might know he wanted to be famous.

Mackay's enthusiasm for the theater was fortunate for Senator John Piper of Virginia City, as an arrangement with the millionaire prevented any loss on bad performances. With Mackay's encouragement, a new drop curtain replaced the

"Sutro Tunnel Scene," green baize covered the stage, and the old patched parlors were remodeled previous to the great fire. When the Opera House was rebuilt two years later, its lumber came from the demolished Caledonia Works—scene of Mackay's first superintendency and his struggle with "creeping clay."

5

A readiness to bet was also one of Mackay's divertisements—not for what he might win, but that he might thrill to genuine competition. The miners, knowing his flair for wagers, had been attempting for some time to play a trick on the Boss of the Comstock—a "sell" in their vernacular. At last a plot was formed.

Mackay was acting superintendent during one of Fair's absences and, as such, spent most of his time in the mines. This particular day he was in the Con Virginia, watching the scattered six hundred athletes stoping out, mounting ladders from crib to crib, carrying heavy planks across scorching rocks, balancing on uncertain piles of ore, blasting, shoveling, sweating in an atmosphere that had brooded there for unnumbered centuries, breathing heavily the oppressive, lifeless air that engulfed them like a hot steam bath.

Completing his tour of the many stations, Mackay boarded the cage and was hoisted to the surface. He washed in the "dabbling tub" provided for the workmen, then entered the Con Virginia office. To his amazement, his paymaster was on his knees measuring the distance between two chalk marks. Mackay's eyes further enlarged as a grasshopper sailed past him. Before he could speak, the employee ventured to explain the situation.

"John, here's a hopper that can outjump any I've ever seen. Let me show you."

"Where did you get him?" Mackay inquired with interest, just as if grasshoppers were an essential part of the office equipment.

"On the side of the mountain," managed the fellow in pursuit of the elusive insect.

Finally captured, the grasshopper was encouraged by a smart rap of the measuring stick to produce another leap. Once again chalk marks decorated the floor.

Mackay was unimpressed. "Why, I can locate fifty grasshoppers that can beat yours."

This was exactly what the paymaster had anticipated.

"Oh, no you can't, John. They aren't made with better muscles than this one."

"I'll make a bet to that effect. But give me a week to find my champion," the superintendent spoke with enthusiasm.

In a few hours, all of Virginia City was informed of the challenge and the proportions of the stake. Mackay had no time to scour the desert hillsides for bugs of any sort, but he engaged the services of two old miners. "Comb Slippery Gulch and the neighboring hills for the broadest jumper in Storey County," was the order. Spurred on by a promise of half the winnings, in addition to their week's grubstake, the men made an unprecedented collection of big, well-fed grasshoppers.

The lode had been busy meanwhile giving expert advice to each of the opponents. One of the Con Virginia chemists proffered Mackay the secret information that a bit of ammonia, sniffed preceding the attempted jump, would make the performing grasshopper exceed all normal attempts. He remembered this, and as soon as the hundreds of insects were brought to him, he conducted a few private experiments. The results were amazing! Even the most sluggish of the lot lengthened his jump considerably after a whiff of the magic fluid.

The date of the contest arrived, both gamblers confident of victory. A jolly crowd of men gathered to witness the exhibition. The paymaster chalked off the starting line. Each had selected his grasshopper.

"You first," obligingly offered Mackay.

His friend placed his jumper on the floor, and gave it a quick rap. What a leap! The audience shouted its approval. Confidently Mackay brought forth the challenger, gave it a good whiff from a small bottle in his pocket, and placed it on the chalk mark. Grinning in anticipation, he barely touched the grasshopper's legs. The insect made a feeble hop, then fell over in a stupor.

Surprise and chagrin crossed Mackay's face in quick succession. What had happened? The onlookers were hilarious as he made out a check for the amount of his loss, for his puzzled expression was very funny. Mackay bided his time until all had left for the Crystal Bar to celebrate. Then he stepped to his store of grasshoppers, selected another big fellow, and placed the opened bottle to the feelers of the insect before making it jump. Again the same disastrous results. He repeated the performance a second and third time with others. What could be the matter with the ammonia? He raised the bottle to his nose. Chloroform! No wonder there had been so much interest in the wager. The dignified Bonanza King, caught looking foolish, made a story worth repeating in laughter-loving Virginia. Mackay was able to laugh at himself, so remained on the same friendly terms with the inspired paymaster.

10   Tongues on Wheels

1

John Mackay's troubles began in earnest with the advent of 1877. "Bear" interests had fed and fanned the flame of doubt and dissatisfaction which had already been engendered among Bonanza stockholders by the suspension of Con Virginia dividends, the transfer of portions of its ore-crushing facilities to the California workings, and the drop in market price of the stock of both mines to forty-five dollars a share. Had the bottom of the treasure been reached? Criticism of the Big Four arrived at the acute stage.

The *San Francisco Alta* championed the Kings of the Comstock:

The attacks on the Bonanza mines and venomous falsehoods on the part of newspapers and vindictive malice of individuals are invoked in aid of unscrupulous stock speculators, who for nearly a year have persistently exerted themselves to ruin the market value of the most extensive mining properties the world has ever known. In this, they have been but too successful.

Not a day has passed but the air has been filled with rumors that the mine is played out and the last dividend paid. Lying so-called experts made pretended visits to the mine, and by false representations induced the stockholders to sell. The consequent weakening of the price caused others to let go.

It will be observed that the managers of these mines give their whole time, abilities and experience to the benefit of the stockholders. Messieurs Mackay and Fair are always in the mine. The former gentleman—though his fortunes are counted by tens of millions—is himself *damnati ad metalla,* devoting himself with singular conscientiousness to the welfare of the stockholders, being in the mine from early morn to night.

The other gentlemen, notwithstanding the vast private business

102

incident upon their great wealth, devote their time to the interests of the Comstock.

These men have set the example of how a great property, which may be called a public trust, can be managed to the best interests of all.

The most annoying individual among those who were dissatisfied was a certain Squire Dewey, a onetime crockery merchant of New York City, later a San Francisco auctioneer. Through shrewd investments he had risen to a place of prominence on the Pacific coast. He was considered a "solid man" and as such went to Paris for a holiday. During his absence, the Big Bonanza was discovered. Upon his return to San Francisco he hastened to James Flood, determined to get in on the excitement and wealth of the great discovery. The financier advised him to buy Con Virginia shares. By 1875 this stock had made him an immense sum of money.

With unaccustomed wealth came the craving for power. Dewey looked about him for an opportunity and suspected that it lay in the failure of the Bank of California. His friends whispered that he was being considered for the new directorate. To insure success with the bank, Dewey's fired imagination told him to denounce severely the Bonanza firm.

Then came the great October fire in Virginia City, and the cry rose: Will the Con Virginia pay its dividends? In a paroxysm of fear, Dewey went to the company's offices.

"How much money has the company on hand?" he demanded of the astounded clerk.

"Less than one-half million," was the latter's honest reply, not mentioning the unparted bullion.

To Flood the terrorized Dewey went. It was Flood who had persuaded him to buy the stock originally. It was therefore up to Flood to save it.

"When will you get up the new hoisting works and raise ore again?" Dewey questioned the unfriendly Bonanza King.[1]

"If the shaft is on fire, it will be a long time," Flood replied. "If not, in forty to fifty days."

"Will the Con Virginia pay a ten-dollar dividend this month?"

"I can't say what the trustees will do," Flood answered impatiently.

Shrewdly, Dewey decided he could profit by this disaster. With no dividend apparently forthcoming, he would sell his divident on 15,000 shares at $5.00 a share to some unsuspecting person, and collect a harvest of $75,000!

When he learned his disastrous mistake—the mine having paid a ten-dollars-a-share dividend in spite of the fire— Dewey began to write letters to the *Chronicle*, voicing his opinion of the Bonanza firm. In spite of his slanderous statements, circumstances continued to prove them lies.

Then he made a proposition to the Bonanza Kings, offering to cease his attacks against them for the small sum of $30,-000 or, better still, for the purchase of his 1000 shares of Con Virginia stock at $80 apiece, albeit the market price was but $50.

Flood expressed the opinion of the quartet. "I don't consider that Dewey's friendship is worth $30,000!"

2

At the annual meeting of the Con Virginia Company, held at its offices in the Nevada Block on January 11, 1877, the attack against the Bonanza Kings was launched.[2] Entrenched in a corner by the window overlooking Montgomery Street were Mackay, Flood, and O'Brien. Their advisor, Solomon Heydenfeldt, was close at hand, ready for action.

About them were massed the discontented stockholders, sponsored by Squire Dewey and James White representing the English investors.

John Mackay answered the demand for information regarding the developments in the mine. "As far as the managers of the mine keeping back information, I have not done so, and I believe Flood has not. All the information about the mine was included in the superintendent's weekly reports, which are open to the public."

Though Fair had noted by exhaustive letters every drift, winze, upraise, crosscut, drill hole, the extent of the ore bodies, the character of the ground, and prospects in view, Dewey started an argument: "You managers have not denied the reports of withheld information over your signatures. If you had done so, the public would have believed you."

Flood did not move from his chair as he answered, "I have not withheld any information that I was able to give. I think I know the reason for Mr. Dewey's attack on me. He is an enemy of mine, and came here expressly to insult me."

"That is false, sir, and you know it!" Dewey cried.

"It is not false," the financier retorted with irritation. "You have said in the street that you had lost $70,000 on this stock, and that you intended to hound me until you got it back."

Dewey was becoming more agitated too as he shouted, "That is false too, sir. What I said is that I have lost $50,000 by a falsehood that you told me, sir, and. . . ."

"I'll have that back in your teeth, sir!" Flood exploded, jumping to his feet.

"Come, come, gentlemen," Mackay interceded. "If Mr. Dewey will gamble in stocks, he must expect to lose once in a while; and, at any rate, this is no time to bring up personal matters.

"I want to say now—and not only for the benefit of Mr. Dewey, but all the gentlemen here present—I am the largest individual stockholder in the company, and have more at stake than any man in it. I work the mine with Mr. Fair in Virginia, and it is simply impossible for us to tell two or three days, or a week ahead, what the mine may develop. We cannot promise anything for the future to a certainty. Events are constantly happening to upset our calculations. Hard rock, caves, bad air, and a hundred things occur at any moment to retard our progress. The management have done as well as they can, and can do no more."

The disgruntled stockholders were not interested in the ever-present threat of floods, parting cables, weakened shafts, or broken machinery. It was the two-dollars-per-share dividend about the middle of the month, the addition of three million dollars to their accounts—appearing like magic from the labors of the miners—which occupied their attention. Consequently they were gullible when wreckers, bewailing the dividends paid others, invented canards regarding bullion shipments and future developments.

Mr. White of England now took the center of the room. He was a distinguished-appearing gentleman with long hair and the air of a revivalist. Sixteen years in Parliament were his sole recommendations.

He too complained of the policy of the Bonanza managers. England was dissatisfied with the secretive course they were pursuing. It was quite inconsistent with British frankness.

This statement was too much for John Mackay. "No Englishman could know anything about the working of an American mine—a matter regarding which even Fair and I might be mistaken. Why don't these people who think they know so much about the mine come to Virginia and try to run it themselves?"

There was no answer to this, but Dewey continued to heckle him.

"Now, my dear sir," Mackay checked him, "if you will come up to Virginia, you shall have all the information you can possibly get. I will give you every opportunity to examine the mines, pay your expenses, and furnish you with all the wine and cigars you can consume. Come up with me! I'm going back in a day or two, and shall be glad to have your company."

Laughter covered Dewey's confusion as the Bonanza Boss continued to refute other arguments presented.

"Mr. Dewey says that the assessor in Virginia informed him that a mill would pay for itself in two or three months. Now I would like to know from whom he got that information. No mill can be cleared short of a year or eighteen months. You cannot build a mill that will crush three hundred tons of ore for less than four hundred and fifty to five hundred thousand dollars.

"There is a great deal of talk about tailings. We will sell them if anybody wants them. These tailings ran to waste in the Carson River for ten, twelve years, until Mr. Hobart and myself conceived the plan of running them down to Big Flat and saving them. The plan cost one hundred and thirty thousand dollars. As I have a very large family (meaning the miners), my object in taking them down was *to give them to the little fellows to work when I am gone.*"

John Mackay revealed more in that sentence than his audience suspected. ". . . when I am gone." By that he meant when the last bit of treasure had been removed and he was no longer a part of this world of extremes; when the black and white of a self-centered kingdom had turned to gray premeditation; when this life he loved so well was exchanged for the electric atmosphere of his wife's salon and the company of men whose motives he could not understand.

Already he knew that the message of the lode would be forever in his heart, and that he would find it impossible to quit him of the loyalty, responsibility, and devotion he felt to a true and faithful consort—the tremendous fissure of the Comstock.

But there was no place for dreams or reflection amid the antagonism of greedy stockholders.

3

Far more formidable to Mackay was the battle with the eternal opponent, Nature, the ruler of Mount Davidson, with its weapons—water and heat. The Hale & Norcross and Savage mines were below the 1,900-foot level and still sinking their shafts. In many places the miners drilled, blasted, and removed ore for weeks at a time from below the surface of the water without ever seeing bottom.

The heat was so great in the lower levels that the men had to take turns on the picks and power drills. The temperature was 154 degrees! The hot vapor contained so little oxygen that only a few men could work in the face of the lowest drifts. Five minutes of work—ten minutes at the most—then half fainting, they would stagger to the cooling room, a section made tight and supplied with fresh air from blowers on the surface. Tons of ice were used daily.

The deeper the work was pushed, the less employment there was. Mackay was forced to discharge men frequently. Dividends were not forthcoming. It took strong nerves to hold up under the curses of the disappointed stockholders and public.

James White, representative of the English investors in the Comstock Lode, accepted Mackay's heated invitation to visit Virginia City. With his mining expert, he carefully inspected the Bonanza mines and mills and left for England some months later, completely satisfied as to their management.

Mackay promised a resumption of Con Virginia dividends in May. The ore on the 1,650-foot level of the mine should mill $300 a ton, he said. When assayed, it fell far below one-third of the anticipated valuation. Ore that paid $89 a ton net in 1876 yielded only $45 a ton profit in June of 1877. Production must, therefore, be twice as great to maintain the former dividends.

Protests from the public continued in spite of a reduction in the cost of milling. It insisted on a drop in production costs as well. The managers were accused of having caused the market depression. It was up to them to restore the confidence of a public that whispered of barren ground ahead.

Colonel Fair cried doggedly, "Hard times are past. Affairs will soon brighten up."

The stock market, however, remained demoralized, aggravated by a serious threat of reduction in miners' wages. Both

Mackay and Fair opposed any cut in pay, but pressure was being brought to bear from every side.

Five of the Bonanza firm's mines on the north half of the lode appeared to be exhausted—Sierra Nevada, Gould & Curry, Savage, Hale & Norcross, and Chollar-Potosi. Ruinously manipulated, the Ophir mine also had failed to meet expectations. Though the public in general had been seriously bled, Sharon was one who cashed all his Ophir stock before its collapse.

4

In May of 1877, John Mackay bought a ticket for Paris, hoping that by dropping the ballast of Comstock worries for a few months, he might escape the doubt and cynicism attempting to invade a nature intended to be kindly and unspoiled. The crown was becoming heavier and heavier. Yet this trip to Europe was to prove more expensive than the millionaire imagined.

There was a tinge of gray in the neatly parted brown hair of the forty-six-year-old mining magnate who stepped off the train at Washington, D.C. He wished to visit the Chief Executive before May 17, because, at that time ex-President Grant, having completed his second term of office, would sail on the *S.S. Indiana* for a tour of the world.

Mackay was still concerned about the demonetized silver dollar. With the government planning to resume specie payment in 1878, there was considerable dubiousness in the minds of many as to the country's ability to handle the load. The millionaire wished to assure the nation's statesmen that he would take $100,000,000 worth of the bonds required to sustain the $346,000,000 in greenbacks, should occasion arise.

Nevada's senator, John P. Jones, saw to it that no such necessity occurred. In February of 1878 his efforts to make silver more than mere merchandise resulted in the passage of the Bland-Allison Act, declaring silver once again legal tender, and insuring the purchase for coinage of not less than $2,000,000 worth of silver monthly by the treasury, and a possible purchase of $4,000,000.

Though the wealth of the Comstock was once again wanted for coinage; this act succeeded merely in retarding the fall in price; it did not provide for the consumption of the great surplus of metal on hand. In 1879 there would occur a further drop in silver due to the prolonged depression of trade in Germany and the United States. Ninety-six cents per ounce was to be its coinage value, when $1.29 was the rate the Comstock demanded.

In 1881, with England and Germany refusing to abandon the gold standard, the bimetallic movement was destined to take the form of national agitation within each country. In the face of the increased supply of gold in the world, it would be impossible for the United States to keep up the price of silver.

5

If John Mackay thought he could keep his private life separate from his public one, he was mistaken, because the social efforts of Mrs. Mackay, entertaining in a style unequalled by any private individual in Europe, forced him to shine in reflected notoriety. Thus his arrival in Paris in 1877 was announced in the French newspapers as an important event, and mention was made of the fact that he had engaged apartments at the Hotel Anglais, his wife being out of the city at the time.

Relating his experience three years later, Mackay said, "When I arrived at the station, I was therefore not surprised to have a fine-looking man walk up, ask my name, and request me to be seated in a carriage ready to be driven to the hotel. This person saw to my baggage, rode upon the box, and escorted me to the hotel register, which I signed, my conductor in the meantime holding a blotting pad over the name of the hotel at the top of the page.

"When I turned away, he said, 'I trust, Mr. Mackay, you will find the Hotel Grand to your liking.'

" 'But I don't wish to stop here,' I said much annoyed. 'It is the Hotel Anglais at which I am expected.'

" 'Is it possible?' spoke the stranger. 'A thousand pardons. I was not aware that you had a preference. How stupid of me.' "

Whereupon the Frenchman hurriedly called a coupé and had Mackay transferred to the other hotel. The incident was forgotten, but Mackay recalled it with vividness six months later when a bill of enormous proportions reached him in Virginia City. The proprietor of the Hotel Grand demanded the cost of five months' lodging plus wines, etc.

"You see," Mackay recounted, "the rascal had gone back to the hotel, passed himself off for me, and lived thereafter on the fat of the land, giving wine parties every night. Whenever the bill would be sent in, he would put it off on some excuse or other, until suspicions were excited, and the landlord sent the register around to the Nevada Bank's Paris agency and had my signature identified. That made matters all right again until the fellow left, when he actually had the gall to direct that the bill be sent to my address over here for collection!"[4]

This was one account John Mackay refused to pay.

The lonely heart of the millionaire was always susceptible to adventurers since he did not fully understand design. It was not easy to retain that inborn sense of decency and a generous nature in the face of deception and ever-present treachery. He was even a bit naïve at times—a characteristic that endeared him to his ostentatious wife.

Life had become heavy in the mountains of Washoe without his family, but life was too confusing here in Paris. Though love and devotion persisted between husband and wife, the old intimacy was gone—buried in the confusion and profusion of levity and effulgence, dulled by a scintillating array of rich hangings and myriad-faceted candelabra. The heart of simple John Mackay was left empty and void of feeling.

6

Mrs. Mackay was occupied with plans for a reception honoring General Grant that would startle even the most extravagant of Paris hostesses. On October 24, 1877, the former president was to arrive from London. This entertainment would result in her acceptance by the inner circle of French society; of that she was certain.

To aid her was Mrs. Lucy Hooper, wife of one of Grant's appointees, Robert Hooper. She assisted Louisa Mackay in planning her entertainments and in selecting those to be invited. Being a newspaper correspondent, Mrs. Hooper used the press to call attention to this new hostess. In return, Mrs. Mackay paid her a regular commission, and rewarded her by numerous gifts, the most valuable one being a pair of solitaire diamond earrings.

John Mackay was not present at Grant's dinner, where the menus were framed in gold instead of the accustomed silver. There were a thousand persons at the grand reception following the dinner, and favors for the ladies at the ball were reported to have cost one hundred dollars apiece.

Of interest to the world the day following the dinner was not the magnificence of the entertainment, nor the fact that musicians from the *Opéra* had been engaged to play while the guests met the flashing hostess.

The story that rocked art-revering France was that the "Bonanza Queen" wanted to have the Arc de Triomphe, located opposite her mansion, illuminated in honor of the plowboy president. She had asked the municipal authorities for the privilege, gossip insisted, and when refused, told them she could buy it if she wished and illuminate it whenever she took the notion.

Alas for Mrs. Mackay! The vision in the public mind of thousands of gas jets burning from the celebrated monument, of Roman candles and rockets exploding over Victory and her war chariot, was a death blow to the carefully nurtured plans of Mrs. Mackay and her social secretary. Whether spoken in jest or seriousness, this reported arrogance, at a time when she was struggling for that cherished entree into the select French salons, resulted in a closing of those doors to her and a noisy turning of the key in the locks.

7

John Mackay had intended to return to the Comstock the middle of July, 1877, but his wife insisted that he accompany her to the small seaport town of Trouville, France, for a holiday. Not until September could he resume his miner's life.

There was but one noticeable change in dusty Virginia— Sharon had added a cherry-colored passenger train to the Virginia & Truckee Railroad. The lode was still a nursery for San Francisco millionaires. The two Bonanza mines, Con Virginia and California, yielded three of the monthly four million dollars' worth of bullion, and 1,150 of the 2,500 tons of ore that rose daily from more than a quarter of a mile below the earth's surface. The Con Virginia alone, by October of 1877, had given more than $33,000,000 to the wealth of the world. Its glory was nearly over, for the men frequently ran into dry digging.

Adolph Sutro sat jubilantly in his office—the front rooms of his two-story mansion—knowing that the Burleigh drills were penetrating the heart of the lode, furthering his tunnel. Eighteen thousand feet in by October of 1877. Only two thousand feet more to go. He continued to promise speed in drainage and a great saving of wood, machinery, and labor by his project.

"Why pay Sutro four thousand dollars for what costs us only three hundred dollars to hoist?" Mackay asked. "With the finest machinery in the world, we can handle the water—but ventilation is a problem, of course."

When floods stopped all activity in the Savage mine, Fair and he became more agreeable to compromise. Little did Sutro realize that it would not be until the end of June, 1879, that the mines would begin to use his tunnel as a drainage adit.

John Mackay assumed the superintendency of both mines and mills of his firm the middle of October. Fair was in need of a rest. The constant care of ores, roadways, water, timber, men, and machinery was gigantic. The nine mills crushing Bonanza ore could not begin to handle the supply of rock before them.

Mackay discharged miners until this surplus had been somewhat reduced, but hired additional men at the mills to handle the very valuable slimes. More than one million dollars' worth of ore was unavoidably lost every month on the lode through lack of adequate chemical and mechanical processes. Still, in spite of the shortcomings, production for 1877 rose to $36,301,536.

Of the twenty-five Comstock claims, thirteen were under the control of the Bonanza Kings at the close of that year. Ophir, Mexican, and Union Con had been added finally to the old guard—Utah, Best & Belcher, Gould & Curry, Hale & Norcross, Savage, Caledonia, Yellow Jacket, California, Con Virginia, and Sierra Nevada (Johnny Skae's pet).

All were worked on one general plan, thereby making a saving of one-third in expenditures. The mammoth C. & C. shaft was down 1,880 feet. Each day $17,000 were spent for timbering the underground city, $6,000 a day for firewood to drive the steam engines, $2,000 for quicksilver, $1,000 a day for ice. Figures . . . dollars . . . and rumors.

8

"Bonanza King as Kingmaker!" was the caption of an article in the *San Francisco Chronicle* of December 3. Five men—John Mackay, Mr. Forney, General Badeau, Dr. Evans of Paris, and Mr. Childs of the *Philadelphia Public Ledger* were credited with a scheme to establish Ulysses S.

Grant on the Bulgarian throne! This was at a time when his supporters in the United States were promoting a third term for him.

"Grant has not known of it, except in a general way through Badeau," confided the *Ledger*, "but thinks he will be favorable to it. The matter will be settled at the great capitals of Europe. Mackay is willing to spend a large sum for the legitimate expense to bring it about."

Men of extremely reserved temperaments, the two principals—Mackay and Grant—did not even listen to such a ridiculous proposition. Grant's heart and soul were in America.

In the trail of this story appeared others equally provocative to the imagination of the West. "Bonanza Mackay is to become Il Conte di Mackay by purchasing an Italian dukedom," gasped the January 7, 1878, issue of the *Gold Hill News*. An Italian nobleman of Scotch-Irish descent!

"He is to purchase a Papal earldom and set up a titled aristocracy of his own," the *San Francisco Chronicle* elaborated the following day. "Of course, then Mrs. Mackay will be countess. Only think of it, you millions of American women, whose husbands bear only the plain title of Mr., or Colonel, or General, or Governor, or Senator. To be a count or countess means business. It is getting a title that will last a lifetime and can then be transmitted to one's offspring. How much better for an Irishman to thus raise himself above the vulgar horde of his countrymen and ally himself to the nobility of the Old World."

With this report, the imagined fortune of John Mackay increased. Estimates which had formerly ranged from four to one hundred million dollars, were now given as two hundred and seventy-five million. The Duke of Westminster had a fortune of only eighty million. Rothschild had but two hundred million. Without moving a finger, it would seem that Mackay's wealth had increased 800 per cent overnight! No wonder he confided to his friends that a person who wanted more than two hundred thousand was foolish.

The wealth of the Bonanza Boss retained its exaggerated stature due partially to the announcement in February that he was to purchase the baronial mansion of the ruined stock manipulator, Baron Albert Grant, in Kensington, a western borough of London. This would appear to be but a step toward the high estate of purchasing a title from His Holiness the Pope, whispered San Francisco. Plain John Mackay, who had never had nor wanted a title, saw himself the target of a sarcasm that he must accept with dignity or ignore with complete indifference. The farthest the lode had ever gone was to suggest, jokingly, that Mackay be called "Reverend."

San Francisco forgot that Nevada boasted more generals and colonels than the regular army of the United States; that every person who had ever held an official position—whether it be that of attorney general, schoolteacher, dancing master, or prize fighter—demanded a title, and clung to it to the end of his days.

Kensington was Mrs. Mackay's conception of a home—a mansion for the site of which two hundred houses had been demolished by Baron Grant. Its grounds covered seven and one-half acres on a line with the Royal Palace, directly opposite the famous Kensington Gardens and in an exclusive and aristocratic section of London.

The tragic aftermath of Ulysses S. Grant's reception in Paris had been responsible for Mrs. Mackay's desire to change residence. Her new home was composed of one hundred rooms and apartments with domed ceilings, panels of mother-of-pearl, gold borders, walls of arabesques, oak and walnut everywhere—massive, original, allegorical, of cool splendor and impersonal glitter—a flaunting, flashing sumptuousness that no Comstock miner would enjoy. Here one would have to be careful of drops of wine and ashes from fine cigars. Virginia City looked good to John Mackay.

A haunting feeling of nostalgia crept over him as he saw the change that had taken place in the mining town. With physicians of renown, lawyers of great ability, and professional men of talent in every line, the Comstock knew how to be at home in the best of society.

Simplehearted Washoe was gone, and with it had gone loved ones and home for Mr. Mackay. With it would go a part of him, when the great bonanza was no more. Already the Washoe zephyrs, busy collecting little mounds about the roots of the sagebrush, whispered of dying things. When quartz turned to clay, and the treasure of the ancients was scattered across the world, where could John Mackay find new contests to satisfy his driving ambition?

9

Forces other than human agencies were conspiring to break the dominance of the tetrad of mining zealots. On May 2, 1878, the death of William O'Brien occurred. Mackay paused in his preparations for departure to Europe; Fair returned to San Francisco from Paso Robles where he had gone for treatment of his rheumatism; Flood shelved the many lawsuits against the firm.

O'Brien's partnership, begun with James Flood on Nelson Creek in Plumas County, had been given legal recognition a short time before his passing. This notice had started serious contemplation as to whether Mackay and Fair were still in the company, or whether this was a mutual declaration of the independence of the two teams. A year and a half before, all the firm's property, excepting mining stocks held in common, had been divided among its members.

O'Brien's estate of twenty million dollars went to his two sisters, four nieces, and three nephews. His worth to the firm came from his ability to make friends. Subjected to the close scrutiny of an envious world, the others had profited by the urbane qualities of this member.

The funeral service, conducted at Calvary Cemetery in San Francisco, was a simple one. Flood and Fair were among the pallbearers. Where was John Mackay?

Not from lack of respect was he absent from this group, but on account of a shrinking from public notice that was fast becoming an obsession with him. He had striven so hard to show others how worth-while he really was, how he had climbed above the shadows of his associates in his own peculiar direction. But the spotlight he had gained was oppressive to his innate shyness and subconscious feeling of inferiority. Not in business matters, not in battling man or nature did this trait appear, for work gave him a self-confidence that knew no confines. Only in large social contacts, only before the acclaim of what he felt to be an insincere world, was he miserable.

Could the spontaneous homage of his few close friends keep him natural and kindly? As age came, would his rugged nature completely withstand the shocks of mounting criticism, notoriety, deception, and blackmail? John Mackay was stepping cautiously in this fairy-tale land, where in five years the four partners had piled up $150,000,000. In comparison, Gates, Carnegie, and Schwab were slow to gather their royal wealth.

At the time of O'Brien's death, the dividend of the Con Virginia was cut to one dollar a share and its main shaft closed for repairs. Would the story of the silver rush to Washoe end as abruptly as it had begun? Fair had issued a proclamation in February attempting to revive the old life of enthusiasm for the Big Bonanza.

"My son," he said, "the baby's born, and it's bigger than its daddy!"

Conjectures ran riot among the stock speculators as to where the baby bonanza was, since Fair had shrewdly neglected to disclose its position. Mackay knew that if there was a nursery holding another wonder baby on the lode, Fair's "fine nose for ore" would detect it.

The silent, insistent forces of nature were the only serious threat to Mackay's secure position as suzerain on a shell of a mountain. How much longer, he asked himself, could the great diapason of Mount Davidson give forth sounds of rushing activity?

To the inquisitive lode, Mackay summarized the situation as he saw it prior to his departure for Europe.

"During the remainder of 1878, the California and Con Virginia will yield two million dollars' worth of bullion a month, but the poverty of the lower levels, the intense heat, and the great flow of hot water below the 2,400-foot level are increasing production costs. The ore assays eighty dollars a ton but it costs twenty-eight to remove it."

10

The international exposition in Paris displayed a choice selection of ore specimens from Nevada and California, Mackay having prepared and shipped the twenty-three cases representing his state. Through his liberality, California was able to send an exhibit of twenty-two cases.

According to an irate Californian, the gift came about in the following manner:

The California Legislature has peremptorily refused to appropriate any money to defray the expenses of having that state credibly represented in the Paris Exposition. But what is astonishing is the fact that the merchants and brokers of San Francisco failed to respond liberally to the call for contributions to aid the commission to prepare its specimens and send them to Brooklyn for shipment.

At a meeting of the gentlemen having the matter in hand, it was decided that the attempt to have California represented at the World's Fair must be given up for want of funds.

There was, however, one man on the Pacific Coast who was not willing to have our mineral resources made conspicuous by their absence at the Exposition, and who preferred to defray all the expenses from his own purse. That man is Mackay.

As soon as the news of the Commissioners' action was made known to him, he telegraphed them to proceed with their mineral collection as quickly as possible and charge all expenses to him.

This private munificence of Mackay should put to shame the Legislature of the Golden State and insure the finest exhibit of minerals which the coast has ever made. The gift is a gift to every mining man on the Pacific Coast. A citizen of Nevada has done what the whole state did not have the public spirit and generosity to do.[5]

The Bonanza King had moments less charitable and more amusing. Just before he left for New York in May, a lady paid him a visit in Virginia City. During the course of the conversation, she expressed the great desire to see a photograph of John William, Jr.

"Really, Madam," the millionaire replied with gravity, "I would be glad to accommodate you, but the atmosphere of Paris is so bad that they can't take photographs."[6]

He had apparently learned something from James Fair.

Still the *Sacramento Bee* had this to say of Mackay: "He has none of the airs of a monarch. If you happen to know him, he will say a few pleasant words and bid you good morning. His demeanor is invariably quiet and modest, and the most jealous eye can detect no bluster in it. Mackay is not an educated man, and knows he is not."

Perhaps this was the secret of his popularity.

11

Though the exposition opened May 1, 1878, John Mackay did not arrive in Paris until June 6. To greet him were his sons, four and eight years old, and a new brother-in-law, Count Telfener. This former intimate of King Humbert had married Mrs. Mackay's sister, Ada Hungerford.

A description of Mrs. Mackay at this time is as follows:

She was as good a patriot as the best of us. She was simple, easy, unaffected as her husband—who always has the air of a mere friend of the family; and it was quite on the cards that she might vote Paris frivolous on a first inspection, and hurry away from it in disgust as soon as she had seen the sights.

She carried her simplicity to the point of having no figure to speak of, she had a good deal of natural shrewdness, she talked well because she did not try to talk wittily, and her face was pleasant to look on because she had the good sense to let it take care of itself.

She would condescend to mention people and places on the other side, and she really did not seem ashamed of the tie of race between herself and Webster and Washington.[7]

The Mackay silverware, just completed by Tiffany & Company at a cost of $150,000, was one of the many indications that Mrs. Mackay was changing. The nine huge boxes, especially constructed for this service of one thousand pieces, required thirty-six porters to convey them in one trip to the Tiffany exhibit at the exposition.

Two hundred men spent one year in the manufacture of this monument to the wealth of its owner.

To put as much silver into it as possible, as much work on the silver as possible, to impress the beholder with the enormous cost of the service and the skill of the makers, is the effect of this large accumulation of coin and cunning. The form chosen is called Indian. Indian or not, every dish is puffed and swollen so as to get the largest possible surface for ornamentation. Every square inch of every dish is covered with minute repoussé work—flowers, foliage, figures, a running riot.[8]

With a strong contempt for any outward display of wealth, Mr. Mackay soon decided to return to the United States. Everything in Paris was too puffed and swollen for him.

"Mackay came to the Comstock so quietly yesterday," stated the *Gold Hill News* of October 18, 1878, "that no one knew of his presence there except those immediately in business connection with him. He was reported 'not in the country' to callers at his room last evening (International Hotel), but was at his usual place of business today."

There was work for him on the lode, more work than ever.

Fair had resigned as superintendent of the Bonanza mines; his rheumatism was becoming very painful. W. H. Patton, former assistant, had replaced him. With Mackay back, Fair left for New York City. Troubles followed him there, too. He was confined for some time in the Windsor Hotel with boils.

One would have expected John Mackay to desert the fading Comstock since there were no more bonanzas to work, but, instead, he took his place beside Patton, assuming the superintendency when the latter became ill. Colonel Dan Hungerford, stopping off for a visit in November before continuing to Mexico for the winter, was astounded at the accusations hurled at his son-in-law. Mackay was said to have remained at the mines in order to insure a Republican victory. His enemies maintained further that the large force of men hired at the mines would be discharged immediately after the election.

With the two Bonanza mines still stubbornly owing the $100,000 in penalty on delinquent taxes since 1874, the cry for payment was renewed at this time. The Bonanza Kings had had nearly two years of grace provided by a stay of execution. No matter that the mines were no longer paying dividends.

This fight continued through February of 1879, when lobbyists began working for and against the kings before the newly organized legislature. A Bonanza Relief Bill had been introduced. This bill, and the one submitted the following year, were cast out, but with typical perseverance the firm tried again in 1881, at which time they succeeded in electing a body of legislators who released them from the tax penalties—a truly undeserved success.

There was grief somewhat less deserved for the kings from an old source—Squire P. Dewey. As soon as the Con Virginia Company applied to the United States government for a patent on its 711.027 linear feet of the lode, he started one bogus suit after another. There were claims for ten feet of the Con Virginia, forty-eight feet of the White & Murphy, claims for the restitution of four, five, ten, twenty-six, and thirty-five million dollars to the stockholders. Dewey had published a 78-page pamphlet purporting to expose the underhanded dealings of the Bonanza Kings.

With no encouragement from the courts or from his many published attacks, Dewey offered to sell his one thousand shares of California stock to the Bonanza firm for $52,-600—the amount claimed to have been lost through false information—and be friendly with them.

Flood answered for the company. "If there were no other objection to his proposition, that last part—his friendship—is sufficiently objectionable to make me reject it. I might stand the money part to get rid of him and send him off to Paris, but to have his friendship inflicted on me is a little too rough!"

The trials continued through October of 1878 until everyone's patience, including that of the United States Circuit Court, was exhausted. However, after five years of newspaper abuse on the part of the *San Francisco Chronicle* and two years of litigation with Squire Dewey, Flood and Mackay decided to make a settlement and end the affair. The terms of their compromise were not made public.

11   President and King

1

It was July of 1879. Heat waves were hovering over the
long fissure, sucking the tart and pungent perfume from the
sage. A tremendous quietude shrouded the Comstock Lode.
The Bonanza Kings had compromised with Sutro—the "King
of the Indominatables," "Bullheaded Assyrian," the "Tunnel
Maniac" whose drain had been completed July 1.

All tewnty-four mines had signed an agreement with him
for the use of the tunnel, a perfect triumph of engineering
skill and mechanical ingenuity, of co-ordinated brain and
muscle. It was for the benefit of the mines, but alas! there
was only a murmur in the heart of the Comstock.

John Mackay returned to Virginia City after five trying
months in San Francisco. A blackmail suit against him had
surpassed in scandal the amazing press accounts of "Mrs.
Bonanza Mackay" in Paris.

Stated the *San Francisco Chronicle* of February 13, 1879:

The suit of William H. Smallman against Mackay of the Bonanza
firm, claiming $200,000 damages for the destruction of the plain-
tiff's domestic peace and the violation of his marital honor, with
the collateral suit brought by Mr. Smallman for a divorce from
his wife, Amelia, is attracting considerable attention as an enterprising piece of litigation, and is likely to excite a much greater
degree of interest if ever brought to trial. At least half a hundred
persons are liable to be called upon for information and advice to
assist the jury in reaching a fair estimate of the damage incurred
by the reckless conduct of Mackay. . . . In the aggregate, the case
embodies probably the most stupendous, complicated, and multi-
tudinously distributed scandal ever developed in the annals of the
American courts.

According to the press, Amelia Smallman had had a most colorful career. Claiming she had lost one husband due to Mackay's attentions, her studied witchery and perpetual smile enabled her to captivate a second husband, the English-born purser of the Occidental and Oriental Line. In order to be with his bride, William Smallman resigned this position to become clerk on a bay steamer.

A short time after the marriage, however, Mr. Smallman swore that John Mackay began to persecute his wife because she would not leave him to become the millionaire's mistress. His outraged feelings demanded that he seek revenge outside the law, but, upon second thought, his unfamiliarity with American customs persuaded him to seek redress in the courts. With evidence of Mackay's guilt so direct, conclusive, and damaging as to promise to prostrate the court, Smallman averred that two hundred thousand dollars in damages was a moderate price for virtue.

In his complaint, the clerk further stated that Amelia had been driven hopelessly insane by the perfidy of the Bonanza King, a fact which physicians would substantiate.

It was not long before doubt began to rise in the minds of San Francisco readers as to the truth of the affair. They saw Amelia Smallman continue her promenades as the "perambulating sensation" of the city, without any noticeable loss of two hundred thousand dollars' worth of virtue. Reporters, who called on her at her O'Farrell Street apartment, were met by a gay and charming woman in black silk evening dress, who gracefully manipulated the long train of her gown.

The police knew a great deal about Amelia Smallman. A few months before this, she had been brought before the court on the accusation of a swindled Englishman. Her vivacious wink, "which recovered itself like the opening of a morning glory," and her soft voice, did not have its expected effect on the sedate judge, who was concerned only with the two thousand dollars entrusted her by the gentleman for investment in mining stocks.

When Mrs. Smallman was unable to produce any evidence of the disposal of this money, the court ordered her to return half of the amount in cash, and tender the Englishman a note for the balance.

To obtain one thousand dollars in cash for him was not difficult. Mrs. Smallman got it from hard-working Mary Tack, housekeeper at the Grand Hotel. Convincing her that her savings of one thousand dollars could be greatly increased through mining investments—since Mrs. Smallman had inside information from her intimate friend, John Mackay—the clever woman obtained the money. However, as soon as the Mackay scandal broke into print, Mary Tack demanded the return of her one thousand dollars.

With infinite resource, Mrs. Smallman took immediate steps to pacify her.

"Now, Mary, my broker said to me this morning, 'I see that you have borrowed $1000 from poor Mary Tack and haven't paid her. You must pay her immediately, before I can do anything more for you. When you bring me a receipt from her, showing that her money had been returned, I will let you have the $3000 you require (to fight this new case).' Now, I have brought the receipt, Mary, and all you have to do is sign it. Then I will go down and show it to my broker, and draw the $3000, and come back and pay you the $1000 out of it."[1]

Simple Mary Tack affixed her signature to the release before a notary public, conveniently placed in an adjoining apartment, and that was the last she saw of Mrs. Smallman.

The swindling young woman did not stop there. In October of 1878, she and her husband had spent an evening with Mr. and Mrs. Cooper of 33 O'Farrell Street, letting drop a chance remark that a new bonanza was about to be revealed on the Comstock. Mr. Mackay, desirous of terminating their love affair, had given her the priceless information as a parting gift, she elaborated. This was occasioned by that fact that certain parties in America had written an anoymous letter to Mrs. Mackay, revealing the secret of their affair.

The Coopers were intrigued. "What is the name of this stock, now worth only fifteen dollars a share?" they asked her.

But Mrs. Smallman would not tell them. However, if they wished, she would buy them some stock through an agent in New York, since Mr. Mackay had made her promise that she would not buy stock in San Francisco. An investment of five thousand dollars would multiply to forty thousand dollars in no time, and when Mr. Mackay returned from his visit to the Paris Exposition, he would assist her in handling the matter. By making a lot of money for her, Mackay would consider himself free of all obligation. It all sounded plausible to the Coopers.

On May 14, 1879, two days before John Mackay took the witness stand in his own defense, the trial of the Coopers against the Smallmans for grand larceny occupied the municipal court. "The indictment charges that the prisoners in April last obtained $2000 from William Cooper and his wife, Margery, on the pretext of investing it for them in stocks, and that thereafter the money was misappropriated. Mrs. Smallman, through her standing with John Mackay, had obtained various sums amounting to over $6000, and then invested it for her own benefit."[2]

Mrs. Smallman's lawyer, Mr. Tyler, claimed that this case was instigated by Mackay himself, who had had his secretary, George Wells, search the Smallman apartments for a certain affidavit he had made to reassure Amelia's mother of her daughter's integrity. Being unable to locate this paper, the defense continued, Mr. Mackay had threatened Mrs. Smallman with ten years' imprisonment.

The Smallmans' story on the witness stand was that they had planned to take their fortune, made from the new bonanza, to Dublin—Mackay's birthplace—and from there contact him on his frequent trips to Paris in order to continue the profitable speculation. The money which the Coopers had given her, Mrs. Smallman stated, had been sent to Virginia City for Mr. Mackay to invest, and the sum sent to New York for purchase of stock through his agent there, had been transferred by Mackay to San Francisco.

Supported by the testimony of her maid, Amelia Smallman charged that the millionaire had confided to her in 1876 that the Yellow Jacket would be the coming bonanza, but to wait for a year or two before buying stock. It was at a later date, therefore, that she invested the $2000 of the Coopers and $1,500 of her own.[3]

The fact that the Yellow Jacket mine was a pet of Mackay's did not help the millionaire here, since he had great faith that it would eventually produce a bonanza, and constantly poured money into it, even though he received no returns.

Upon Mr. Mackay's return from Europe in 1878, the young woman claimed he called on her at the Palace Hotel, and then advised her to purchase shares in Ophir, Mex, Utah, or Union Con. These investments also had proven disastrous, she said.

The one person Amelia Smallman had underestimated was John Mackay. He made no attempt to buy her off, and on May 16, 1879, took the witness stand to deny the various stories of giving pointers, etc., swearing that at no time had he, directly or indirectly, communicated any information to either husband or wife.

The great notoriety given the case came to an end on June 22, with the conviction of the Smallmans—one for perjury, the other for blackmail. A new trial was denied and each of the infamous pair was sentenced to four years in the state prison. The mildness of the punishment appeared to be an agreeable surprise to them, but John Mackay seethed with rage for a long time over the baseless scandal. To relieve his feelings, he turned his attention to the discouraging mines.

The mineowners were struggling under burdensome taxes and the financial drain of costly machinery and wood. Hundreds of thousands of tons of low-grade ores could be utilized if the cost of labor were reduced one-half—that Mackay knew.

When the reticent "Boss" finally consented to define publicly his position on the labor question, the news item concerning it was captioned, "John Mackay Talks!" With great reserve he stated that he was quite willing to accord to others what he had always demanded for himself; he was a miner and believed in a fair day's wage for a fair day's work. Even though he could put ten thousand additional men to work in the mines and mills if wages were cut to two dollars a day, he wished it understood that he would do nothing to force down the price of labor.

Mackay spent his days in the tunnels and stopes, or behind the cashier's window, helping pay off the employees. There was a prevailing gravity on his face. He was concerned over the bleak future of the Comstock. The dividends of the two Bonanza mines had been cut to fifty cents a share. The lode was waiting for new developments on the 2,400-foot level of the Ophir. Perhaps this would be Fair's "Bonanza baby."

Fair disembarked from the S.S. *City of Sydney* on July 23, concluding a trip to the Sandwich Islands with his son James, and Richard Dey. San Francisco was not eager for his reappearance.

"When Colonel Fair comes to town, stocks invariably go down," the speculators chanted.

The former superintendent assured everyone that the present discouragement among mining men was uncalled for. The lode put little credence in his statement, for he had used speech so long to conceal his real purposes that it had become a recognized failing. Overindulgence in talk had made the word of James Fair unreliable and ambiguous. Through words, he had spun a confining web about his influence.

John Mackay had been wise in suppressing his thoughts, in decrying any claim to prophetic power. Fair was old and broken in health at forty-eight years of age. He was withering and losing his magnetism. The partner who took a trip to Colorado with Philipp Deidesheimer immediately upon Fair's return was a very different sort of person. His carriage was upright, his movements brisk and virile, his bearing dignified and natural. He was ripening.

2

Noon . . . cool, dry, sunny. . . . John Mackay approached the office mansion of the Savage Mining Company on D Street. His eyes traveled from the roof with its silken streamer bearing the inscription, "Virginia City, Nevada, October 27, '79," to the front door, with the word "Welcome," formed of red, white, and blue flowers. Evergreens, and garlands of roses and camelias flanked the entrance. Bunting covered the outer walls.

Within, the chandeliers, picture frames, and brackets were completely hidden beneath smilax, and the mantels were burdened with bouquets of the choicest flowers on the Pacific coast. Mackay's eyes lingered on a center table in the parlor, its plate mirror top supporting a huge letter three feet wide and six feet long—a capital "G." The simple miner, who once admired a general, stood as an uncrowned king to welcome a former president. The Comstock had been good to him.

Oblivious of the others hurrying about him, not hearing the cough of James Fair who was recovering from a serious sore throat, Mackay removed his watch from its pocket. Twelve forty-eight. Whistles began to shriek, bells clanged, the Bullion dump echoed with cannon salutes. Ulysses S. Grant was riding Sharon's railroad into Gold Hill.

Mackay knew the order of events because he was on the Committee of Arrangements for the entertainment of his friend. The Carson Guard would descend first, followed by Governor Kinkead and his staff. Last would appear a short, round-shouldered man of fifty-seven years, no gait, no manner, no gold lace, in tow of Judge Richard Rising and Colonel M. G. Gillette. Mayor Young would say, "We are not so pretentious as the great cities, but our hearts are as open, and we remember and appreciate your services to our country." Grant would mumble a scarcely audible, "Thank you."

The thoughts of the Bonanza King were shattered by the flurry of a coach-and-six at the door of the mansion. Mrs. Grant was leaving the carriage, assisted by colored attendants. Theresa Fair greeted her and performed the introductions. In a moment the general arrived with the governor and the mayor of Virginia City. A brief handshake and the party hurried to the east balcony to review the procession of which the members had been a recent part.

Martial music sounded the length of the Divide for the Washington, Emmet, Sarsfield, Montgomery, and National Guards to continue the parade. Two thousand school children lined Main Street as far as its junction with B and C Streets in Virginia, their songs and waving flags giving life to the dry hillsides. Gold Hill had outdone Virginia for the honor of the most flags per square yard. Up to the very last moment the miners had strung gay banners at the shafts from smokestack to smokestack. Superintendent Deidesheimer had set up a regular main and topmast at the Hale & Norcross. The veterans were marching for their leader. The Pacific coast pioneers were honoring the ex-president. Even the Piutes, naked and painted, and very amusing to Grant, lengthened this procession—such a one as the Comstock had never organized before.

General Grant spoke from the balcony: "Fellow citizens: I am glad to meet you here today, and I feel under many obligations for the fine reception you have given me. It is impossible for me to make a speech on this occasion. I am not like your senators who are in the habit of making long speeches to you and catching your votes."

There followed speeches from Senator Jones and Colonel Fair, and the presentation of a seven-foot flag made by Mrs. Gillette. Then the endless handshaking started. At 4:00 P.M. Mackay requested that this stop; the guest of honor was becoming very tired and everyone was hungry. Lunch with plenty of old wine was waiting in the dining room upstairs.

As the sun set over Mount Davidson, the flag flying from Fair's sturdy pole on its peak shone with a glowing halo of light, a spectacle seen only once before—on the eve of the fall of Vicksburg, Grant's great work. With the increasing wind, the flag straightened out and the sun's mellow rays on the rich colors of the banner formed an almost supernatural phenomenon for those below in the dark shadows of the mountain. This was the sort of thing the Comstock liked.

Shortly after nine o'clock that evening John Mackay escorted General and Mrs. Grant into Piper's Opera House through the upper Union Street doors. There were several ladies and gentlemen in the party. As the audience caught sight of their general, it rose to its feet to applaud and cheer. Grant bowed a sober acknowledgement, took his place in full view of all, and the curtain ascended for "The Magic Slipper."

The following evening Mackay brought the general and his wife once again to Piper's, this time to witness the Colville Opera Company in the extravaganza, "Babes in the Wood." In its endeavor to please, the cast overdid both performances, but extremes were no novelty to the Comstock.

3

At ten o'clock on the morning following Grant's arrival, Mackay escorted a party including the general, Mrs. Grant, their son, U. S. Grant, Jr., Mrs. Gillette, Governor Kinkead, and Mrs. Fair, through the Con Virginia and Yellow Jacket workings.

Recounting this visit later to Eliot Lord, Mackay said, "He told me it was the most wonderful sight that he had seen in any part of the world, and that I might be proud to be the master and director of the greatest mining enterprise on earth. That did touch me. Any man might be proud of that, coming as it did from Grant's mouth, which never slopped over."[4]

This was the first and last time that Eliot Lord heard Mackay express a word of gratification in his own work.

Dining at the residence of Senator Jones that evening, Grant whispered to Mackay that he was happy to find lacking the French bills of fare. Mackay's eyes brightened as he added, "It's quite a novelty these days to find a menu in English." At the banquet given in Grant's honor in California—those of Senator Sharon and Mr. Crocker—the former president had been forced to ask someone to translate the menus, as confusing to him as the seventy-course dinner he had had in China.

The Comstock made the little general feel more at home here than at any other place on the coast. Nevada knew how to be a good host. Grant's modesty had endeared him to everyone. While in Germany, Prince Bismarck offered him a review which he declined saying, "I am not a soldier but a farmer." Mackay's respect and affection for an upright and honest man was to endure up to the time of Grant's death in 1885. The general's reverence for success and money made him cling tenaciously to the millionaire.

4

Ever since April 27 of 1879, when Mackay and Fair paid a visit together to the town of Sutro, the lode had suspected that the tunnel would become Big Bonanza property, with Superintendent Patton replacing Adolph Sutro. Fair had been taking the credit of the tunnel project for some time.

"Sutro simply came in and worked upon our ideas," he maintained.[5]

In February of 1880, with continued surmises voiced regarding the disposal of the tunnel property, Mackay expressed himself.

"We want neither Mr. Sutro nor his tunnel!"

In its own new slang, the Comstock was "off its chuck." The project looked unprofitable to Mackay, but shortly thereafter other parties paid one million dollars for the drain. Sutro wisely retired to the Heights overlooking Seal Rocks and the Pacific Ocean. In 1894, he would become San Francisco's mayor.

The Big Bonanza was now a great throat in the mountains of Washoe, its bottom 2,400 feet below the surface. Seven years after its discovery, the lode returned to *borrasca*.

Though Johnny Skae, who had gained independent control of the Sierra Nevada mine by a secret combination with members of the Anglo-California Bank, cried, "Strike!"—and succeeded in inflating his stock from $20 to $85 in August of 1880, the fabulous bubble burst, and James Flood was hard put to sell the shares at $40 in November.

John Mackay's life was still tied to the Comstock, and even though he said dully, "It's a poor man's pudding," he purchased Flood's interest in the mines for five million dollars. Why did he insist upon taking an active interest in the mines when someone else might have been entrusted with their direction? The king's confidence had been abused too often for him to express his thoughts completely. The early reserve of a miner had developed into the stony silence of a millionaire—not sulky or ill-tempered, but sad and inscrutable in his dignity. He confided to his friends that there was a fascination to this mining game which caused him to spend long hours in the perilous and exhausting work. But that was not the entire reason.

Mackay had no illusions regarding the future of the lode, but he was determined that as long as the mines could pay for the extraction and milling of their ore, work must go on—work for those needy men who had spent their best years in the underground hall of courage.

The occasional dividends during 1880 from the Big Bonanza were from surplus accumulations obtained from the milling of Fair's "baby"—an ore body located on the old stopes of the 1,500- and 1,750-foot levels, low-grade ore passed up in the tumultuous days of glory. The 130 tons of ore daily rising at this time through the C. & C. shaft were sufficient to pay running expenses.

"I have a very large family...." Mackay had said. "... the little fellows...." He hesitated to entrust these mines to anyone else. That was his reason for staying. His loyalty to the miners was as intangible and persistent as the zephyrs of Washoe, his fear of failing them as real and unreal as the heat and hell of the lower levels.

5

Fair was touring the world, accompanied by his son James, and Irving Scott, manager of the Union Iron Works where most of the firm's large machinery had been built. Theresa Fair and the other children—Charles, Theresa, and Virginia—remained in San Francisco, having moved in June into their new Pine Street mansion.

Kindly, pleasant-faced Theresa Fair, who had contributed much energy and sound business judgment to the early firm, found herself more and more in the background as her husband expanded in importance. She was to receive a divorce in May of 1883.

The later years of him who "did not intend to lead a poor man's life" were to be more barren and hollow than the hills of the desert which had caused James Fair to bloom. Fair would be lonelier by far than Mackay, who sat in his two-story brick home, constructed after the fire, with only servants for companions.

Fair was now broken in health and in mind, O'Brien was gone, and Flood was ill. Only Mackay had the vitality to carry on the immense burden of the underground run. He considered leaving for Europe in July of 1880, entrusting the management to Frank Osbiston. Yet he was loathe to go. Perhaps he had a premonition that his usefulness on the lode would soon be over. A trip to Yosemite sufficed.

Even this vacation was shortened by the arrival of Ulysses S. Grant, Jr., in the West. Mackay met him in Reno and accompanied him to San Francisco. After a fortnight in the bay region, the miner returned to Virginia City alone. Another chief was on the way—President Hayes was to visit the lode on September 6.

Though all good Democrats were urged by the *Virginia City Chronicle* to give a "cutting rebuke" to the President, the Comstock could not resist an opportunity to display its flags, pull its whistles, and ring the fire bells. The Chief Executive received a noisy welcome, after which his party descended the C. & C. shaft under Mackay's guidance.

Mrs. Hayes and the other nine ladies in the group each received a silver brick beautifully inscribed, together with a specimen granulation of silver. Mr. Taylor of the Con Virginia made the presentation—after the tour was completed—at the request of John Mackay. The latter disliked such ceremonies, especially when ten women were the recipients.

Mackay knew that Fair would be back September 28 with the usual questions for him:

"What are you doing here? Where are all the men? Going to sleep all along the lode?"

And Mackay, who was described at this time as "tolerably stout and increasing, straight as a pick handle, wears a new twenty-dollar suit of brown jeans, a heavy mustache, no spectacles, looks jolly enough when not bothered, talks little, and doesn't give a damn," would just look at Fair and place a few questions of his own.

12   Backstairs' Influence

1

"This thing of a state being represented in the U.S. Senate by a silver brick is getting monotonous," complained the Republicans of Nevada, using an expression of Mark Twain's when the announcement was made that William Sharon intended to carry the party's senatorial standard for another six-year term.

"The throwing over of John W. Mackay, who is a bona fide resident of the state of Nevada, and the cordial endorsement of William Sharon, who is a resident of California" at the Austin convention, held in May, 1880, seemed incomprehensible. During 1879 Sharon had drawn no salary as a senator, being more occupied with his affairs in the West than with his duties in Washington. Though the interests of Nevada probably had not suffered from this irregularity, a more conscientious representative was desired.

"Why is Mackay a good enough Republican whenever funds are required, but unworthy of recognition whenever party honors are to be bestowed?" everyone asked.

Those who knew him realized that it was not his heavy monied interests alone which had induced him to refuse once again the candidacy for the senatorship. It was not the fact that his presence in the West was of more direct and tangible importance to the state of Nevada than a seat in Washington. The Bonanza King scorned special recognition from his party. He was content to remain a controlling influence in the organization.

Surprise was even greater when Mackay was not a delegate to the Chicago convention in June of 1880. Surely he must have wanted to work for Grant as the presidential nominee.

"I do not care to go," he insisted. "Heavy business cares and responsibilities occupy me here, but if James Blaine is nominated instead of Grant, I will do as much as any man in Nevada to elect him."

Neither one received the nomination. It was James A. Garfield. He too would become a friend of the "Bonanzanaire." Mackay had a way with presidents.

Rumors traveled from Paris that the other half of the Bonanza duo had aspired to political office. Could it be that Fair, who had never participated in politics, who had voted only for Douglas and Cleveland, had now consented to run for the senatorship? For years he had given his check to the Republican Central Committee, since he believed generally in the policy of this party regarding finances. Yet Fair was nonpartisan, and the Democrats had been communicating with him in Paris, seeking permission to place his name on their ticket.

Fair continued to refuse the offer until the Democrats began to pour into his ears the disagreeable things Sharon had been saying regarding the proposed candidacy of his enemy.

"You have talked too much," Fair said to Sharon upon returning to the lode, "and I will warm your little jacket for you as sure as you live! I had not intended to run, but now I am resolved to be Senator, and you are the first one I am giving the information to."[1]

Fair's political popularity was evinced by his reception on the lode following an eight months' tour of the world. On September 28, a long line of carriages took his dust from Steamboat Springs to Virginia City, the old stage driver, "Curly Bill," guiding the four-in-hand which brought Fair up Greiger Grade past the many mines decorated with flags in his honor.

Mackay was at Fair's home, once again surveying an evergreen arch of welcome over the entrance door. If Fair announced himself a Democrat, it would be difficult for Mackay to support both his party and his partner. Theresa Fair had pleaded with Mackay to assist her husband in winning the nomination and the election. It would mean so much to the children. The prestige of a father in Washington, D.C., could be of great social significance. Apparently the Nob Hill home of Mrs. Fair had not attracted the choice sections of

San Francisco aristocracy. Mackay had promised her he would do all he could.

Now he watched Fair alight. With an honest-looking smile, Fair paused before the crowd. Gray streaks had found their way among the curly black hairs of his head and heavy beard, and his weight had increased from 170 to 207 pounds. The Big Bonanza had made him fat, satisfied, constantly amused, too tolerant, too smooth, too balanced.

"Speech! Speech!" the miners cried.

"Not now," Fair refused genially, his large hazel eyes lighting up his entire face. "I'm not much of a talker anyway. I prefer to let my actions speak for me."

"Well, we're glad to see you back anyway," someone cried.

"I believe you are," Fair responded. "You act like it."

Mackay stepped forward to greet him. The crowd sang "Home Again" and "The Sweet By and By," then made a rush for the champagne and cigars.

With only one month until election, Fair would have to work fast. His enemies were legion, and the many threats against his life had caused him long ago to replace the knife in his bootleg with a good, concealed revolver. The lode which praised him to his face and cried enthusiastically, "There goes Fair!" every time he drove about in his light single buggy, cursed him when the spell of his dynamic presence faded.

Could the mining superintendent who claimed no party allegiance defeat a staunch Republican, Sharon, backed by Senator John P. Jones and the wealth of John Mackay? Nevada, in senatorial elections, had always been faithful to the Republican party. Yet Mackay knew that the Comstock remembered that Fair was a man of great ability, a leader highly cognizant of his own power, an unsurpassed practical, as well as scientific, miner whose health and youth had gone into the vast underground run. It would be loyal to him, Mackay was certain.

Flood got busy in San Francisco when he heard that Fair was running against Sharon. Stocks had always played a part in Nevada's political campaigns, an active market being made the leading feature.

"Aha! Now we shall have some fun," the stock operators cried eagerly.

With Fair controlling the votes of hundreds of men in the many Bonanza-firm mines, and Sharon's subordinates in charge of Belcher, Crown Point, and Chollar-Potosi, the lode quivered with suppressed excitement in anticipation of the general election. Mackay knew that the discovery of a new ore body would guarantee the winner of this election. Every job the Bonanza firm offered meant a vote for the men pledged to Fair. These men, if elected, would be duty-bound to vote for him as senator to Washington.

The Democrats engaged all the bands in both Gold Hill and Virginia City for the entire time until election. When the Republicans sought musicians, there wasn't a one to hire.

The Nevadans were not concerned with an election "on the dead square," for they had unblushingly bought and sold votes for years. Ten dollars was considered a fair offer for any vote. Often clubs offered a joint sale of votes. How much money changed hands at this contest was uncertain, but Fair's liberal expenditure undoubtedly placed most of the Democratic legislature in office.

Therefore, when the state legislature met in Carson City, Fair was greatly surprised to learn that Adolph Sutro had declared himself a Democratic candidate for the United States Senate. During the campaign his name hadn't even been mentioned. After some uneasy moments and considerable conniving on the part of James Fair, the Nevada legislature met and Fair's undisputed victory was announced. A great many Republicans had joined the Democrats to give him three-quarters of all the votes.

Up to the very last moment, Fair would not declare his party allegiance. Forced to do so on March 4, 1881, upon entering the Senate chamber, he announced himself a Democrat. Actually, he remained nonpartisan.

The horizon about coolheaded James Fair, now called "Uncle Jimmie" on the lode, was widening. With no conscience or sentiment to trouble him, a complete rift with his wife came when he moved to the capital. He had refused to take her with him.

Mrs. Fair could never hope to scale the heights to where Mrs. Mackay already stood. Her struggle grieved John Mackay.

2

Samson was shorn. The Big Bonanza was played out. At the time of Fair's departure for Washington, the two mines, once worth nearly $10,000,000, rated at only $1,700,000. In the aggregate, the lode had dropped from a market value of

$262,669,940 to $6,905,580. All that remained of the Con Virginia hoisting works was the boiler room. Women and children with sacks and baskets were plundering the ruins for firewood. Virginia no longer had a city government.

Immediately following the November fifth election, John Mackay, too, made preparations for departure. It was not easy to desert these diggings—the only home he had known for twenty years. He would miss not only the physical activity of the mines but the relaxation of the opera house, where so many times he had sat on the stage while some Irishman "held forth."

"How long will you be gone, John?" Harry Rosener asked him, as he drove the millionaire in a four-in-hand to Reno.

"Maybe two—three years," was the reply.

His friend laughed. "I'll be expecting you within a year, John. You don't know how to be absent from the Comstock."

Any sort of boom would certainly bring him back from Europe. Life would be dull in Paris. He who had spent his life in sharpening a pick would not be happy in refashioning his life in the salons of Europe.

The youth who strode so eagerly into Washoe in 1860 was departing a score of years later in a private car taxed $1,620 for the coast-to-coast trip. Mrs. Pullman had prepared her palace car for Mackay's use to New York.

His fortune was rated at fifty million dollars, surpassed only by those of Vanderbilt, Astor, Gould, and Sage. Still, the small boy who had had dreams of greatness was not satisfied now. Conflict was in his blood. Where was there offered another stirring battle such as Nevada had given him? Mackay was determined to climb still higher.

On December 3 he was in Queenstown, Ireland, having sailed hurriedly from New York City after a few hours' visit at the Fifth Avenue Theatre where John McCullough was playing an engagement. Social New York was not even aware of Mackay's presence, a very perplexing and absorbing problem having occupied its collective mind. Should the "four hundred" admit to their charmed circle Sarah Bernhardt?

London was more concerned with the millionaire. "What is the future of the Bonanza mines?" he was asked from every side.

"There is nothing new I can say, further than add that all that men and machinery can accomplish is now being done in their development. I am hopeful, and that is all I care to say. I don't wish to mislead or confuse, and *were I to talk much I* would be misconstrued and blamed as I have been so often before. Time will tell all."[2]

There Mackay expressed coherently that fear of being misunderstood that had ever tortured him. His "don't give a damn" attitude was but a bold cloak for a solvent rather than a dominant personality. It had been developed to hide the loneliness in his soul, the need for someone in whom he could place all his trust. Yet, was some of his success due to much that he lacked?

"He is one of the most unselfish men I ever met or knew," Rollin Daggett said of Mackay at this time. "His liberality is something marvelous, but he is averse to let the world know of his generosity. He has given away two times the amount of money that either of his partners has, and that is saying a great deal since both are exceedingly generous men.

"In Virginia City, he mixes with all classes of people freely, and I believe he would rather any day take an old miner by the hand than a millionaire."[3]

3

The recent battle of political parties in Nevada faded as Paris split into two camps—Mackay versus the most noted French artist of the eighties. Mrs. Mackay had commissioned Jean Meissonier to paint her portrait. However, when the finished work was presented to her, she was horrified to see a woman at least ten years older than herself, a veritable caricature of the "Bonanza Queen."

Mackay viewed the portrait and expressed his opinion. "I want a Meissonier, not Meissonier painting a slovenly imitation of Cabanel." He would not pay the 75,000 francs agreed upon in the beginning.

The ensuing court battle was the least of the affair, for the American and French salons took up the quarrel. Meissonier was accused of having produced it after an insufficient number of sittings, of taking no pains with it—since anything was good enough for Nevada—of having painted in Mrs. Mackay's hands from one of his models, of deliberately making a caricature to ridicule American ostentation, of even allowing one of his pupils to complete it.

"The painting is unworthy both of the subject and the artist," Mackay steadfastly declared.

Those who indorsed the work gave Meissonier an elaborate dinner as a vindication. Promptly thereafter, the French press became hysterical when a false report circulated that Mrs. Mackay had thrown the portrait into the fire. To end the publicity, John Mackay made a financial settlement—how large is not certain; but it was some time before discussion of the affair ended.

Mackay secretly hoped that this episode would sour his wife on Paris. He wanted his family to return to New York with him. Already he had purchased real estate in the metropolis—the Stevens property on Fifth Avenue near Fiftieth Street. There he had fitted out large apartments as well as offices. It was apparent that his wife's wealth and hospitality had laid her open to unending attacks from borrowers, blackmailers, social parasites, and stranded Americans. John Mackay had considered settling in southern California, but his wife refused to hear of this suggestion. If he must continue to commute to Europe at protracted intervals, it would be simpler from the Atlantic seaboard.

In the spring of 1881 the Mackay family came to New York, leaving the much-disputed painting hanging with its face to the wall in a small room of their Paris home. As time rendered the episode less significant, Mrs. Mackay would ask visitors to Carlton House, "What do you think of the painting?" And when a guest fumbled vainly for adequate words, she would laugh gaily at his embarrassment.

A portrait of her, painted in 1879 by Alexandre Cabanel, was more to her friends' liking. It did justice to the fair, earnest face, with its lustrous blue eyes.

John Mackay's hopes for the permanent New York residence of his wife proved to be futile. Mrs. Mackay was not yet ready to launch an attack on New York society. She had made her plans for London. Nothing would stop the "Silver Queen" this time.

13   A New Round

1

Always the same vision—Power. With great wealth, new perspectives had opened up before John Mackay. The world was a toy in his hands. Up, ever up, the spring of ambition carried him. He could not stand still after so many years of climbing.

Seated in his New York office, dreams of another spectacular battle fed his imagination. Subconsciously, he was laying out a definite scheme of advance, making exact preparations for the realization of these resolves. It was not long before his loose speculations took on the shape and hardness of belief. This time the contest would be shorter, because he had a more tried and experienced mind.

The exorbitant size of cable bills to his wife had long irritated John Mackay. Investigating the cable system, he ascertained that the men in control of the Western Union Telegraph Company and its appendant transatlantic cables had brought into a "pool" with them all the existing British and French cable lines. With an absolute monopoly of telegraphic communications between the United States and Europe, and without competition, this new clique arbitrarily fixed its rates—charges so excessive that the commercial interests of both continents voiced indignant protests.

The press was loudest in an appeal for a reduction of tolls, the *New York Herald* being the leader of the opposition. Its owner, James Gordon Bennett, Jr., had had his guns aimed at the chief shareholder of Western Union for a long time, exposing one unscrupulous "Gould" enterprise after another. But Jay Gould and the other arrogant monopolists knew that

138

business was at their mercy, and remained as unreasonable as before.

Under the existing conditions, the *Herald* asserted, the "pool" taxed the public to pay for the dividends on the inflated and "watered" stock of its various companies. To make matters more intolerable, the speed of service had become more and more uncertain, and there was no longer any guarantee of privacy of information. News was constantly leaking out. Someone must establish an all-American cable system, based on actual cash cost and managed honestly, to provide accurate, fast service at low rates.

Capital had always remained aloof from the great Gould, firmly entrenched behind his seventy-five million dollars. No individual had ever dared incur the hostility of the multimillionaire. The public was of one mind—that a new company could not succeed. But to John Mackay the mere thought of abolishing the present onerous conditions by a tough struggle had the stimulating effect of a big bonanza. He would form an independent transatlantic cable company, but not alone.

Where in the field of complainants was there a suitable partner for Mackay who was foolhardy enough to ride in the whirlwind that would come? Would the cable's best customer, James Gordon Bennett, be interested in a communications scheme? It would be an ideal association, since the two men were of like feather.

The journalist had just the type of daring and enterprise needed to supplement Mackay's nerve. Not gifted with his father's writing ability, the younger half of the great newspaper dynasty had spent a fortune making news instead of gathering it. He had commissioned Henry M. Stanley to do what the British government had tried vainly for half a century to accomplish—explore Africa and discover the source of the Nile. In 1878, with the African map remodeled and the geographical societies of the world in permanent indebtedness to him, he purchased the yacht, *Pandora,* renamed it the *Jeanette,* fitted it out with men and equipment, and dispatched it in 1879 to the North Pole to study the temperature, surroundings, etc., of the Arctic. Bennett's interest did not necessarily run to science, but he was intent upon giving the world something to talk about, and through these activities he had made himself the most colorful man in America.

Mackay was shrewd enough to realize that he would need a newspaper behind him, since the outcome of the proposed battle would depend a great deal upon public reaction.

Would Bennett be agreeable to a partnership with anyone? He had consistently refused to participate in any commercial enterprise outside his paper. Conferring with the journalist, John Mackay discovered that he was as eager as anyone to promote a new and independent cable service. So far, Bennett had been able to conduct only a verbal war with the powerful financial interests concentrated in the "pool." With Mackay's fortune behind him, he was more than willing to break family traditions.

"You realize," Bennett warned the enthusiastic millionaire, "that this means a long, expensive fight, one involving your private life as well as your public life. The monopoly and its agents will hesitate at nothing. They've already approached me with intimations that the *Herald* will be granted special concessions if I abandon my attacks on them."

The king did not frighten easily. To him, the plan was not only feasible but practical. Those who doubted the possibilities of winning had not taken into account the tremendous force and resolution of a graduate of the Comstock.

On December 10, 1883, the battle lines were drawn with the incorporation of the Commercial Cable Company. John Mackay was installed as president, Isaac Bell, Jr., and Hector De Castro as vice-presidents, David B. Davidson as treasurer, and George G. Ward as secretary and general manager. Twenty million dollars went into the sinking fund, the greater part of it subscribed by Mackay. Two submarine cables were promptly ordered from Siemens Bros., London.

The surprised Jay Gould cried in vain, "There are already too many cables. Any capital invested in a new concern will inevitably be lost. It is only through the formation of the Western Union monopoly and the present charges that the existing cable companies have been able to continue."

2

By 1884 the two new cables across the Atlantic were in working order. The Mackay-Bennett Company announced a forty-cent rate in opposition to the seventy cents per word charged by Western Union. The public was interested. Gould dropped his company's toll to twenty-five cents, with open threats that he intended to ruin his competitors. In retaliation, the new firm lowered its charge to a like amount. Businessmen of both continents began to enter the contest. Their enthusiasm grew as Western Union cut prices to twelve cents a word. What would venturesome Mackay attempt now?

It was a critical moment. Mackay's entire fortune was at stake. He called a conference in the company's offices. One of the directors suggested a six-cent rate for the Commercial Cable Company.

"Impossible!" Mackay exclaimed. "We couldn't last long at that price, as there would be no profit in it. Suppose we place all our cards on the table—announce to the businessmen that twenty-five cents is a fair rate. I'm of the opinion they'll stick by us."

He had not underestimated the sportsmanship of Americans. Following his announcement that there would be no further reductions, many rallied to his support. The very nature of the new service rendered was in itself sufficient to insure the co-operation of commerce. Besides, the public realized that if the independent company was ruined, cable rates would return to the former high. Any man or corporation that disdained to follow the dictates of Jay Gould was a novelty. The experiment became a success when the press and innumerable business houses paid the Commercial Cable Company twice the toll asked by Western Union.

Mackay's purse had lightened considerably. With an elaborate establishment in Paris for Louisa, with children in exclusive private schools, the eighteen months' price war threatened to eclipse his financial wrestle with the Comstock. In addition, rumor placed Bennett under heavy obligations to him, the report going so far as to estimate the journalist's indebtedness to Mackay at two million dollars.

The next move must come from Jay Gould. He offered peace at forty cents a word. The king was uncompromising.

"Mr. Gould," he replied, "our company has discovered that it is able to make a decent profit at twenty-five cents a word instead of the original forty cents. We have no intention of changing."

The financier knew he was beaten. To continue, Western Union was forced to establish identical rates. Gould prepared a parting shot in the form of a personal attack upon Bennett. Copies were given to all New York papers except the *Herald*, but the alert managing editor of Bennett's organ learned in advance of the vicious attack upon his employer and contrived successfully to obtain a copy of the story from the proof sheet of the New York press. Without the consent or knowledge of Bennett, the *Herald* carried Gould's denunciation of him in headlines. It was a master stroke, for the financier was hoisted thereby on his own petard.

3

The fame of John Mackay spread. No longer was he known as the Bonanza King, a millionaire, the husband of a socially inclined wife. He was the man whose iron nerve had opposed a moneyed Goliath throttling the rapid communications of the country. To Mackay, the moral success of the undertaking was of more importance than the financial outcome. Power from the brain that had not been too lazy to study; power from the head that had taken over the work of the hands.

His ideas were still ahead of those he was leading; his new work had just begun; he was still dreaming. With the admiration and support of business, Mackay realized that it was an auspicious time to establish a land line system. The cable would eventually suffer without connecting continental lines. This must be the greatest commercial company in the world. Thus, in 1886, John Mackay organized the Postal Telegraph Company to continue the fight on land with Western Union. It was to be one of his greatest investments.

With wires running to all parts of the United States, scandal soon became attached to the offspring of the cable enterprise. The telegraph company decided to sell out to the government at a large profit, all negotiations for the sale to be handled by George S. Coe, a large stockholder in the firm and president of the American Exchange National Bank of New York. Speculators managed to inflate the stock to a ridiculous figure. Mr. Seney of the Metropolitan Bank of New York was but one of the major gamblers. The collapse of the proposed transaction rendered the stock practically worthless. The Metropolitan Bank, undermined by other unwise investments of Seney, failed. Mackay's fortune, depleted by a recent large investment in one of New York's underground railway schemes, was seriously threatened once again. He managed with difficulty to maintain his control of the telegraph-cable company.

Tarnish was forming on the silver and gold of the Comstock. This new field of endeavor carried a promise of endurance. Mackay had gone to the core of the earth. This time he would girdle the globe with electricity. Such were his present dreams.

14   The Big Kindergarten

1

During those years of New York residence, John Mackay took frequent trips east and west. The visits with his family were far-separated and short; his journeys to San Francisco frequent and long.

Mrs. Mackay had made rapid strides with the French tidewater aristocracy of the Channel. She was not the daughter of a soldier for nothing. She continued to take the offensive until her objective was achieved. Her generosity as a hostess and a customer, and her kindness to struggling art students and impecunious noblemen, gradually erased much of the early French prejudice. One by one the more exclusive salons were opened to her as she became the acknowledged leader of American society in Paris.

Her friendship with Pope Pius IX was one of the distinguished relationships she enjoyed. She was one of five persons honored by the decoration of the Order of the Cross; and after the death of Pius IX, she was sent a pearl-encircled miniature of him. Several months later, on her visit to Rome in March, 1879, the new pontiff, Leo XIII, presented her with other valuable souvenirs in appreciation of her works of charity.

In 1884 Mrs. Mackay leased a villa at Cowes for the yachting season—a preliminary sally to determine British reaction. Not long thereafter, her daughter Eva's engagement was announced, and London society opened an interested eye. Eva's fiance was Signor Ferdinando Colonna, Prince of Galatia, descendant of an Italian family second in antiquity to that of Gaetani di Sermoneta, and prominent in the history of Rome.

On February 11 of 1885 the civil marriage was performed, with the church wedding taking place on the following day in the chapel of M. de Reude, papal nuncio. Only forty persons were invited to the pontifical high mass, but the bridal reception following it was a huge affair, aimed at dazzling the hundreds of fashionable guests. Among those present were Mme. Bonaparte, Count Camonto, United States Minister Morton, Count Menabrea—the Italian ambassador—and the Duke de Cazes. There was no mention of Mr. Mackay's presence at the wedding in the press dispatches sent to the Pacific coast, though he was in Europe for the sumptuous event.

2

Now Mrs. Mackay was ready for her next move. She leased a spacious home in London—No. 7 Buckingham Gate, opposite the palace, and took her first steps within the magic circle of social Britain. Mr. FitzHenry, the Ward McAllister of London's "four hundred," saw to it that circumstances were auspicious.

With everyone expecting a profuse display of the much-publicized Mackay jewels, she made her appearance without even a bracelet as adornment. Her sense of the dramatic was novel to the English. They liked her and showed it.

The Duchess of Manchester became especially friendly with the "Bonanza Queen," and assisted her in making her introductory parties undisputed successes. Mrs. Mackay's grace and vivacity attracted the notice of the Prince of Wales, afterward Edward VII. At a ball given in his honor by the duchess, the prince danced with her many times, and she taught him some of the latest steps. Later, when he received an invitation to a dinner at her home, he readily accepted, since the fame of these affairs had spread from Paris.

John Mackay made an impression on the prince, too. Edward was said to have remarked, after meeting the millionaire, "He is the most unassuming American I ever met."

Common sense had forbidden him to adopt any mannerisms. Though his bearing was dignified, it was completely natural, and his simplicity in dress was noticeable among men of wealth. He would never completely harmonize this new world with the old. The luxuries of London could not be sincerely adopted when the hardships of the Comstock were stippled on his soul. Wealth purely for display held no place in his life.

With British approval of his wife an established fact, Mackay leased Carlton House for her in 1886. Its owner, Charles B. Sanford, was an American whose fortune, made in Argentina, had disappeared in stocks. This mansion was an adequate setting for the elaborate entertainments of London's new hostess. Its art gallery contained valuable paintings; its marble stairway cost $300,000; there was a $250,000 Swedish tapestry on the wall—richness everywhere, velvet reds, deep blues, silver and gold. The social mistakes of early Paris life had taught her much. At last she had the poise so long sought. London would be given no cause for complaints.

Carlton House had too much life and too little peace for John Mackay, yet it was what his wife desired, and that was enough. He purchased it for her in 1891, and had it completely remodeled to suit her fancies. This was her property. Immediate neighbors to the Mackay residence were Lords Pembroke and Brownlow, Home Secretary Matthews, the Duke of Marlborough, Secretary Balfour, and the German ambassador—dignitaries, people of the nobility. Marie-Louise Mackay had attained her life's ambition.

How much the continued attacks of the French press influenced the purchase of this mansion is not known, but preceding the transaction, Mackay began "action for libel through his Paris solicitors against *Galignani's Messenger*. It appears the newspaper published an article charging Mackay with the authorship of certain attacks made against his own family while residing in London."[1] He was forever involved in lawsuits.

Mrs. Mackay conquered New York the same year. Mrs. William Astor, grandmother of Vincent and John, and Mrs. Stuyvesant Fish, corulers of New York's "four hundred," had been considering for some time the matter of the "Bonanza Queen" from Europe. Though she had been lavishly entertained at Newport in August of 1889 by Senator and Mrs. Calvin S. Brice, Miss Leary, and others, the social columns of the *Herald* did not recognize her until January 6, 1891, when her purchase of a box for a charity ball was considered worthy of mention. She had no intention of residing for long at any one time in America. Fifteen years on the Continent had developed a taste for foreign sweets.

3

An apartment on the first floor of the Jessie Street side of the Palace Hotel was Mackay's San Francisco home. There were always good friends awaiting his arrival—Dick Dey, Jerome A. Fillmore, Horace G. Platt, Homer King, Hermann Oelrichs. With them and the members of the Pacific Union Club and the Merchant's Exchange, he could relive parts of that old life he would not abandon.

Mackay still felt an obligation to the desert towns where love and wealth and power had made him a king. Though his mining days were over, someone must provide work for the old fellows still on the Comstock, deserving men whom fortune had passed by.

He could not rid himself of that inner feeling of the lode's productivity. His interest in numerous schemes at Virginia City occupied much of his time and attention while on the West coast. He still retained a few pieces of the baggage of the past. The Nevada Bank was one of the last bonds between two master miners.

Mackay never bothered with the details of the management of this institution; it appeared sound and had earned the confidence of the world through its dealings. When in San Francisco, he spent far more time in the little gymnasium downstairs than in the office of the president. The tellers had rigged out the basement with all sorts of equipment, and Mackay enjoyed watching his employees have their exercise.

In his younger days he had participated in many sports, boxing being his favorite. While others spent their time in gaming and in the pursuit of women, Mackay was seated at the ringside crying, "Bring on your fighters! Trot out your bruisers!" with the other fans of John Heenan and Jem Mace. At the mines, Mackay frequently pulled off his coat before his friends and cried, "Put up your props!" in the hope of sparring a little. Few persons were willing, though, as his bare fists had not lost their hard-hitting reputation.

During Bonanza days he had devoted considerable time to pistol shooting, rapidly becoming one of the crack shots at the Sarsfield Range, but his enthusiasm for fisticuffs had not dwindled. This was shown by his interest in a handsome young Irishman, James J. Corbett, who worked as clearing house messenger for the Bank of Nevada during 1884 and 1885. A friendship immediately formed between the fifty-three-year-old millionaire and the good-humored, stylishly dressed youth who had attracted his attention in the bank's gymnasium. The bank owner was quick to recognize Corbett's natural aptitude for the ring, a combination of marvelous physique and lightning wits that could carry him far in the pugilistic world.

During this time Mackay was frequently approached by young graduates of Oxford and Cambridge who carried with them letters of introduction from mutual acquaintances on both sides of the Atlantic. The chance of having a little fun at their expense was not to be denied, for most of these Englishmen were exceptionally proud of their boxing skill. Corbett had been taking lessons from Walter Watson, boxing instructor at the Olympic Club, and Mackay knew what he could do. Pugilistics being in high favor at the time, it was a simple matter to suggest a few rounds with a suitable opponent. The unsuspecting foreigners were eager to demonstrate their straight left or right haymaker to the wealthy Mr. Mackay. Imagine their surprise when they met Corbett's fast uppercuts and paralyzing hooks.

Mackay's enthusiasm for the fighter increased during the eight months that Jim was employed by the bank. "Why not turn professional?" he asked him. This Corbett did when the Olympic Club offered him the position of boxing instructor. From then on, his reputation as a coming champion spread rapidly.

A three-round exhibition with Jack Burke, English middleweight champion, was arranged for charity in San Francisco, and Mackay was not disappointed in the future "Gentleman Jim," who outpointed Burke. By the time the great John L. Sullivan came to town on one of his meet-all-comers tours, Corbett had become his logical opponent. More handsome than ever in full evening dress, he displayed the finest sparring and footwork ever seen in the West, a type of boxing unknown to the sporting world.

A sixty-round bout followed with Peter Jackson, a Negro from Australia, and the name of Corbett outflashed that of Mackay on the wires of the nation. At the same time, the millionaire watched the performance of his young friend in a very different role. Prize fighters of the eighties invariably turned to the stage for incidental money, but Mackay was not quite so enthusiastic about his portrayal of Armand Duval in *Camille* as he was in his fistic exhibitions. "Pompadour Jim" was headed for New Orleans and twenty-one rounds with John L. Sullivan, yet the paths of fighter and cable owner were to cross again in later years. After Corbett's defeat by Bob Fitzsimmons at Carson City, he would be forced to return to the theater for his living.

4

John Mackay did a little fighting of his own on January 29, 1891, his quick temper causing him to give Mr. W. C. Bonynge a sound thrashing in the president's office of the Nevada Bank. Some months before, the broker had decided to give his family a long holiday in Europe. Business had been good in San Francisco. His socially inclined wife chose London as their new home, anticipating, perhaps, some aid from Mrs. Mackay. In any case, invitations from Carlton House did not appear.

The London press learned of the strained relationship between the two American families and began to publish anonymous stories concerning the dreams and frustrations of the Bonynge family. The broker, who had originally come from England, was said to have been formerly known as Mr. Bunning. Mrs. Mackay was promptly accused of having fabricated all the gossip concerning them.

In retaliation, the old legends about the "Bonanza Queen" were revived and given fresh color. These, quite naturally, were attributed to Mr. and Mrs. Bonynge. The congeries of scandal rolled on to San Francisco, where the two husbands were located at the moment.

It was to be expected, therefore, that when Mackay entered the office of the Nevada Bank and saw his enemy before him, the fighter would come to the surface. Without a word of warning he made a rush for Bonynge and struck him heavily on the jaw. The broker fell, but succeeded in regaining his feet. Once again Mackay delivered a hard blow, and this time his opponent managed to grasp the lapels of Mackay's coat and drag him to the floor. The struggle continued from there.

The sole witness of the fight, I. W. Hellman, made a futile attempt to separate them, but Mackay was intent upon administering a terrific beating. It was necessary for Hellman to call in the bank clerks to pull the two apart.[2]

In the weeks that followed, the accounts of this clash provided further occasion for repetition of the original tales which had started the trouble. Mackay was given innumerable opportunities to regret his rashness.

5

Though still retaining an interest in mining ventures, the Nevada Bank became the pivot of Mackay's western life in 1884. At this time he assumed its complete ownership.

During O'Brien's life, its stockholders and officers had been the Big Four, and Louis McLane had served as president of the institution. Following the death of the first associate, 250 shares were transferred on the books to James Flood, son of the financier, since five directors were necessary. O'Brien had left his bank stock to his sisters, Mrs. Coleman and Mrs. McDonough, but a woman was not permitted as a director.

Subsequently, all of the shares originally belonging to O'Brien were purchased by Mackay, Fair, and Flood. Each then owned ten thousand shares, the original fifty thousand shares having been decreased when it became public knowledge that only three of the five million dollars subscribed by the stockholders had been paid in. Thus, the shares finally conformed with the actual coin deposited. However there were other adjustments to be made.

Bickering began between James Fair and James C. Flood shortly after Louis McLane retired from office on October 18, 1881. Another transfer of stock was made and Flood became president. Relations between Mackay and Fair also started to show strain. By 1884, the three Bonanza Kings realized that still another change was imperative. Finally, negotiations were completed on November 22, and Mackay purchased the remaining twenty thousand shares of his associates.

Here is Senator Fair's statement regarding the reason for this transfer of stock:

Flood came to me and said he wanted to get out of the bank as his health was not good, and because he felt that if he continued to actively manage it in the future as in the past, the result would be to die in the harness.

He made two propositions—the first, that I should buy his shares and those of Mackay, so I could take entire control of the bank—the second, that we should mutually agree to sell out to Mackay, provided he would buy. I accepted the second proposition. Why? Well, for several reasons. I was not exactly satisfied with the way in which the bank had been or was being conducted. My mode of life is not such as to have fitted me for sedentary occupation, and I was not any more anxious to 'die in the harness' than Flood. There were other reasons, but these are sufficient."[3]

A contemporary further elaborates:

In the settlement, Fair claims to have taken railroad property that the other members of the firm looked upon as of little value, and he paid a comparatively small sum of money for it. His management of that property, he (Fair) says, was so shrewd and businesslike, that he disposed of it for a great deal more money than it cost him, and in this, he not only evinced superior judgment to the other members of the firm, but filled his pockets at the same time—both of which were exceedingly gratifying to him.[4]

This strip of railroad, from San Francisco to Santa Cruz, would be more significant later. Fair said it cost him about $7,000,000, including new rolling stock, etc. He was to sell it in three years to the Southern Pacific Company for what Fair claimed to be $8,500,000. Of this amount, $5,500,000 were in bonds.

Though Mackay owned the bank, he did not wish to manage it. He had told Flood in 1875, "If you think it best to organize a bank, I'll go in with the rest, but banking is out of my line. Don't bother me with the details. Just see to it you don't loan money on mining securities."

Formed at the time of the bank's inception, this habit of letting someone else handle the institution's affairs persisted now. James Fair was asked to continue as a nominal stockholder and director for several months after the sale was consummated, ostensibly to assist in the disposal of several pieces of real estate. Flood agreed to continue as president for a year following the transaction. George L. Brander was summoned from the New York agency to handle the office of nominal shareholder, cashier, and vice-president. Once again some stock was placed on the books in Flood's name, and when Fair stepped out, R. H. Follis, brother-in-law of Flood, became one more director-in-name.

This constant resorting and reshifting of responsibility wrote a formal invitation to disaster. Numerous interests, antagonized by the Commercial Cable Company, were kept occupied spreading false reports regarding the Nevada Bank in an attempt to organize breaks in stocks and ruin its backer. Between 1884 and 1886, Mackay discredited countless schemes aimed at smashing the institution, and succeeded in keeping its credit strong throughout the rate war with Western Union. By 1887 he was confident that further vigilance was unnecessary. Fortune and future were once again secure. Though all ready capital had been invested in the new

Postal Telegraph Company, dividends from the heavy investment would handle all his needs. He induced James Flood to buy back into the Nevada Bank. This lessened the financial load so that he might continue at full career with even greater cable projects, even greater plans for his boys.

6

August of 1887 found him in London. He had expected to meet Mrs. Mackay there, but she was in Paris shopping. Before continuing to his family, he decided to visit the bank which was handling the business of his establishment.

The president of the London concern was unusually happy at seeing Mr. Mackay because a matter of considerable importance needed explanation. The banker made haste to broach the subject.

"What business is it that your bank is investing in so heavily at this time, Mr. Mackay?"

"Why, none that I know of, except wheat," the American replied. "We loan money there every fall."

"I've been wondering about it, because the Nevada Bank has overdrawn here to the amount of one hundred thousand pounds."[6]

Mackay was astounded. That meant that the bank was without even working capital. Coming at this time, when his personal fortune was depleted, the overdraft appeared as a catastrophe. Without hesitation, he placed with the foreign bank what securities he had available, wired his family that he must return to the States, and sailed on the next steamer for New York.

This was a race against time, and the fastest speed possible to San Francisco was fifteen days. This was a crisis with greater danger of failure than any other entanglement of his life. He had been caught napping. He had not prepared this battle in advance. What had Flood been doing?

Riding on the horns of disaster did not atrophy Mackay's senses. That calm he had learned among the dangers of the Comstock returned to him as the train pulled into San Francisco. The main thing was to keep the condition of the bank unknown to the public. Any disclosure of the facts would result in a disastrous panic in California.

Mackay hurried down the peninsula to Menlo Park, where Flood sat in a funk, too ill to even think. With his eyesight failing rapidly, and a serious kidney ailment, he had left everything to the bank's manager, George Brander. Mackay learned now that over thirty million dollars had been lent on a crazy speculation. With war threatening between Germany and France, someone had evidently decided it would be highly profitable to corner the wheat market, run the price up to two dollars a bushel, and win giant sweepstakes by selling the grain to the warring nations. The unforeseen fall of M. Boulanger, the French Minister of War who had encouraged hostilities, caused war plans to dissolve, and immediately the wheat market had headed downward.

Neither Mackay nor Flood would hesitate at a corner of this market if success were indicated; but the purchase of California wheat at 30 per cent above its market value and the advance of thirty million dollars on grain had already resulted in a deplorable condition at the bank. All the circumstances pointed the finger of blame at the bank's manager.

With a fortune of at least twenty-five million dollars apiece, it is unlikely that two shrewd and farseeing businessmen would have stepped into wheat dealings so heavily without allowing for possible exigencies. Both had intense pride in their financial establishment. They would not have risked its ruin.

It was apparent that, if they stood in back of the bank, their combined fortunes were liable to be forfeited at any moment. Millions of dollars had already slipped away in the falling market. Further loss was certain, since over forty ships carrying wheat were scattered between Port Casta and Liverpool. If all this cargo were dumped on the market at one time, there would be little hope for either bank or bankers. William Dresbach, handling the sales for the Nevada Bank in Liverpool, had refused to accept further deliveries.

Flood was overcome with self-condemnation because the commission merchants had complained to him shortly before the collapse. "Are you certain that Dresbach's contracts are good?" they had asked. Confined to his home, the most he could do was refer the matter to Brander.

"Don't worry about a thing," the manager had consoled him. "We'll go over everything together as soon as you are well."

So Flood had reassured the merchants. Mackay, too, had trusted Brander. In this, a frequent inability to distinguish between sincere performer and charlatan, his greatest weakness was again revealed.

Mr. Dey, confidential secretary during Bonanza days for

Mackay, and Mr. James E. Walsh, in like capacity to Flood, both insisted that the two owners were in no way connected with the attempted corner. Fair, likewise, placed the blame where it undoubtedly belonged, in spite of the fact that he did not feel kindly toward his associates and besmirched them at every opportunity.

"I think Brander conceived the idea of going into wheat speculations. He may have had a partner on the outside. . . . But for the bank to go into it was just madness. They had everything to lose and nothing possible to gain. . . . This man Dresbach was using their money all the time and they didn't know it," Fair declared without hesitation.[7]

7

Flood was reconciled to the necessity of placing the bank in receivership. There were but $368 in cash on hand to meet the hundreds of demands for payment on wheat. Any one of them could close the doors of the bank. Mackay knew that talent would not save the situation this time. A miracle was needed to resuscitate the once powerful institution. And dollars in hundreds of thousands had to be immediately available.

Bloodhound Fair, nose ever to the wind, had smelled trouble ahead when the mounting wheat prices definitely indicated a pool. He began to make plans for a glorious revenge, expecting that the day of reckoning would not be far off.

The afternoon of September 12, Fair stepped into the office of the bank—smiling, soft-voiced, ingratiating as ever. Mackay was buried in piles of paper, attempting to ascertain how the large reserves of the bank could have been carried out, how even the private property of the depositors could have been hypothecated to furnish speculation money.

"I understand you're in difficulty, John," Fair began with that blandness and tolerance that irritated his former partner.

"D-d-difficulty is right!" was the succinct response.

A horny hand was placed on Mackay's shoulder.

"Well, would three million in cash help? You know, I sold a little piece of property yesterday—that railroad——"[8]

Mackay swung around to face him. "Now, you can save us—it is saving us, that is all. There is no use in calling it by any other name. . . ."[9]

Sentiment was completely lacking between the two, but they had a common pride in the bank. "Slippery Jim" was not above exulting in this priceless moment—magnificent avengement in the guise of charity! Reorganization was completed the next day with Fair as president, owning 10,000 shares, J. F. Bigelow, vice-president, with 250 shares, Flood with 9,500 shares, Mackay with 10,000 shares, and the remaining director, A. E. Davis, with 250 shares.

"I had been thinking about going into this thing before there was a word said to me about it," Fair explained. "I thought the whole thing over, and was conversant with everything about it . . . knew more than either one of them. And they were very unfriendly—in fact, we were all unfriendly to each other. I knew there was no man here who had money enough to save them, expecting myself. I hated to see men, whom I once liked, utterly ruined. . . .

"I got at the books for about three hours, and looked through, and thought I could see daylight for not less than six million dollars. . . . I had the whole thing in my mind. . . . I said 'yes' at night, and in the morning took hold. They didn't know where they were hurt. . . . The complications at that time were simply fearful, and the manager of the bank went right off to England.

"The trouble was they had kept no books . . . and it was difficult to get everything organized and everything satisfactory to everybody. It was an immensity of work. We would sometimes ask other parties for information that we did not want, and in that way, get what we did want to know. You dared not go for the information you wanted, because they would see you were in a hole.

"The very minute I announced I was in, there it was in the paper, and men would walk in and say, 'Is it true, what I have read in the paper?' I would say, 'Yes, it is all true. . . .' Well, they would walk right out, and in a little while, in they would come with their sack. From that time, there were no withdrawals, excepting a little account a woman had of $40,000."[10]

Fair had never been happier.

8

With new capital raised in a short time to augment the million dollars in cash immediately borrowed, the general public was not aware that this great institution, like the Bank of California twelve years before, had gone to its depths and been restored to its former prosperity.

"Big Kindergarten," Fair had called the bank under

Flood's presidency. It had been a nice plaything, a little dangerous, and it had fallen upon them, and would have crushed the life out of them, but he had stepped in and lifted it up.[11]

Dick Dey and James Walsh maintained that it was the divorced wife of Fair who loaned the money that actually saved the bank. Fair claimed that "the bank was indebted to his former wife in the sum of two million," but that Miss Jennie Flood had helped him to the extent of five million dollars—all of which he returned to her in a few weeks.[12]

In any case, credit for handling the actual reorganization of the bank must be given to Fair. It was a critical period, because the ships with their cargo of wheat must be kept at sea until the grain could be sold at proper rates. Fair sold only 2,500 quarters each morning and afternoon, not permitting the ships to land unless he had disposed of their cargo at reasonable prices. By means of the cable, he knew where each ship was, when she sailed, and when she was due to arrive in Liverpool. In spite of forcing grain to remain in demand, Fair was unable to prevent losses amounting to fifteen million dollars. Prices had returned to normal, but the contracts called for inflated rates.[13]

Fair's victory was complete. "I consider that one of the best pieces of financeering I have ever seen done!" are his own words.[14]

Other persons aided in keeping wheat prices up, so within a month the affairs of the bank took on a respectable form. Neither Brander nor Dresbach was prosecuted for the scandalous mismanagement of funds. The incident was closed. Mackay and Flood suffered losses estimated as high as twelve million dollars, but "the Chief" refused to let his nerves sag even after the stretch was over.

"Don't be cast down," he tried to console Flood. "We have lost a little money, to be sure, but we have a little left and we can get along."

The financier of Montgomery Street was too ill to be optimistic. Having been ever efficient and shrewd, the shock of being near bankruptcy left him a broken man. With considerable difficulty his family and friends persuaded him to retire from business in 1888. His 9,500 shares of Nevada Bank stock were entrusted to the care of his son, James L. Flood. A few months were required to put his vast estate in order, so it was spring before Mr. and Mrs. Flood and daughter, Cora Jane (Jennie), arrived in Germany.

Throughout the summer the wires of the Commercial Cable Company flashed encouraging reports of his condition. His health had improved with his travels from one resort to another. The family announced its intentions to spend the winter in Nice. Then, without warning, Flood collapsed in Heidelberg. On October 10, 1888, the second menber of the quartet of millionaires passed on.

Unfortunately he did not live to see the Nevada Bank become the powerful Wells Fargo Bank and Union Trust Company. Flood's name, though, will always remain synonymous with early San Francisco.

John Mackay was to miss his conservative, well-balanced friend.

15   Attempt at Assassination

1

The next years brought little change in the life of the Mackays. There were the usual offers of the senatorship to the Nevada miner, Democrats as well as Republicans arguing that he could best serve his country by holding office. He was as firm as ever in his refusal of party favors.

Mrs. Mackay was a leader of London society, her efforts in 1893 being concentrated in the fight against the revival of the crinoline. While ministers preached against it from their pulpits, and the women of the British capital formed an Anti-Crinoline League in an effort to prevent the adoption of the hoopskirt, the hourglass figure passed.

More serious business occupied John Mackay in San Francisco. He was at the bottom of a scheme to pump out those lower levels of the Comstock mines which had not been completely worked in the reckless days of the Big Bonanza. Not for personal gain did he pursue this idea, but to provide employment for the old Comstockers who still remained there. The evening of February 25, 1893, he intended to take the train for Virginia City to begin this project. Robert Keating, veteran of the lode, was to accompany him.

It was 12:10 P.M. of this day. Mackay was hurrying along Sutter Street on his way to the Palace Hotel where he had a luncheon engagement. As he passed the jewelry shop of A. Hirschman, the proprietor stepped out and joined Mackay in his brisk walk.

"Will you have lunch with me?" the jeweler asked, barely managing to keep abreast with his friend.

"No thanks," Mackay declined. "I won't even walk any

157

farther down the street with you, for if I do, I will be sure to meet somebody, and I don't want to be delayed. A short cut through the alley will be my best route."

He continued his rapid pace and disappeared in Lick Alley, a side street running from Sutter to Post in back of the Lick House, famous for its elegant dining room. This unexpected turn upset the plans of an assassin who had been waiting for the millionaire a few yards farther down the street. He apparently knew Mackay's habit of stopping at Hirschman's store, but had not anticipated the change in route. He raced after the unsuspecting miner, waiting until he was within a few feet of Mackay before he fired his pistol.

The crack of the exploding shell made the millionaire spin about to see his assailant. An old man, with snow-white beard and hair, was trying to aim at him a second time, but the weapon was pointing in all directions.

At the same time, William Prior, employee of the Duffey Brothers' plumbing shop, thrust his head out the rear doors opening on the alley and yelled, "What's the matter?"

Mackay answered calmly, "That man shot me."

Prior was unable to see anyone, as the old man was pressed against the wall, so he stepped out in time to see the smoking pistol pointed in his direction. Without ceremony, he vanished into the store. Another employee, William Williams, had been about to enter the shop from the alley when the first shot was fired. He took refuge behind a wagon.

Mackay continued walking up the alley, keeping his eyes focussed on his assailant. The latter's intention was apparently suicide, but he was having difficulty in aiming. Finally he managed to hold aside his coat with his left hand, and aim at his heart. The hammer snapped several times before the bullet exploded. Mackay continued toward Post Street as his attacker dropped to the ground.

A florist, John Bonner, was the first of hundreds of persons to reach the alley following the attack. He met Mackay walking calmly along while searching for the wound.

"I don't think I am much hurt," the millionaire stated simply, "but if you can drive me to Dr. Keeney's office I will be greatly obliged."

Bonner and William Morris assisted Mackay into a buggy opportunely standing in the alley near Post Street. The crowd made a rush for the apparently dead assassin, thereby making it possible for Mackay and Bonner to depart. Bonner took the reins, but drove rather slowly for fear of jarring Mackay too much.

"Lick him up a little," the injured man suggested, having finally located the wound on his back. "This doesn't amount to much and I can stand it."

In a few minutes, the pair arrived at 14 Grant Avenue, where Dr. Keeney's office was located. Mackay stepped from the buggy unassisted, and took the elevator to the correct floor. Informed that the physician was not in, Mackay requested that he be sent to him as soon as possible, re-entered the carriage, and rode to the Palace Hotel.

2

Already a crowd of friends had gathered about his room on the first floor. Dick Dey, Robert Keating, Colonel Low, and Con O'Connor were among them, deeply concerned over the injury. Mackay firmly refused to permit any examination of the wound until Dr. Keeney and Dr. Morse arrived. Devoid of any apparent fear, he removed his clothing and draped a blanket about him. Everyone was gratefully relieved when the pair of physicians appeared.

"I suppose you're going to cut me?" Mackay asked in an amused tone. "Well, go ahead. I can stand it. It doesn't amount to much anyhow."

"How do you know it doesn't?" the doctor questioned.

"How do I know? Well, I think I have got it located pretty accurately. It didn't make much of a tunnel." He probed a bit on his back with his hand. "There it is. Now see if I'm not right."

One of the doctors produced a hypodermic needle, preparing to administer a local anesthetic, and requested Mackay to lie face down on the bed. The mining king refused to do so, insisting that the bullet hole be probed while he was standing.

The physique of the sixty-two-year-old millionaire was something to admire—175 pounds of muscles and bone as healthy and firm as that of a man of twenty. The spectators held their breath as Dr. Morse manipulated an ivory-tipped steel wire beneath the black-rimmed surface.

"Does that hurt?" the physician asked solicitously as he struck something hard with the probe.

"No, go ahead if you can, but I think that's about the end of it," Mackay answered.

"You are right, and about the luckiest man I ever knew,"

Dr. Morse agreed a moment later. "The bullet is not over two inches from the surface, and as you are not paralyzed, your backbone is all right."

Mackay said simply, "That is encouraging, but I thought as much. The old fellow meant business, and when I first felt that I was hit, I did not know but what he had got me. When he fired, I did not realize that I was hit; then I thought I was hit badly. But on analyzing my sensations and locating the wound, I concluded that it was only a scratch. Say, what are you going to do now?"

"Get it out and have it over in one job," the surgeon responded.

While one doctor held Mackay, the other made four surface cuts low down between the shoulder blades. Mackay did not make a sound until the forceps finally clamped onto the leaden pellet imbedded in the bone. He gave a grunt as the physician pulled.

Everyone rejoiced when Dr. Morse held up the forceps, revealing an unbroken bullet.

"If that bullet had been flattened or bruised, it would be evident that the shot was a severe one. Its smoothness shows that it did not go with much force."

The force of the shot had evidently been spent in the clothing, and instead of cutting the threads of the light tweed coat and carrying portions into the flesh, the bullet had merely parted them. One-eighth of an inch farther to the left, the cartridge would have meant instant death or paralysis.

Dr. Morse insisted that Mackay go to bed, and his associate advised no rich food, no stimulants, no visitors, and no business.

"You two act as if I'm going to die," the patient protested.

"Nothing of the kind," Dr. Keeney denied. "You are not in the slightest danger if you do not run into it; and it's my business to build a fence around you so you can't. Hurts a little, eh? Well, it's nothing to how it will hurt you tomorrow, and tomorrow's pain will be nothing to what you will suffer the next day. The wound is not serious, but it will not be a subject for laughter for the next four or five days, and you will have to remain indoors from ten days to two weeks."

Mackay gave up and went to bed. Dick Dey, his confidential secretary, assumed full charge of everything. When a cable from Mrs. Mackay informed them that she was sailing for America on the next steamer, her husband dispatched the following:

"The old crank that shot me is seventy-three years old. I don't know him and never saw him. The doctor cut out the bullet. There is no good reason for the least uneasiness."

"This cable does not sound as if it came from a dying man, does it?" Mrs. Mackay asked her friends who read the message.

However, she made hurried plans for a trip to San Francisco with her children, even though Dick Dey advised her that she need not come.

In the days that followed, only messages from his wife were permitted to reach John Mackay. The many other telegrams were read and answered by Dick Dey, and in response to all other inquiries, the Postal Telegraph Company issued a stereotyped form of report.

There was one wire, however, which the secretary decided to read to Mackay. Sent from Virgina City, Dick Dey knew that its message was of special significance to the patient:

"Your old friends of the Comstock, which include the large majority of the population, congratulate you on your providential escape from the bullet of the assassin, and hope for your speedy recovery."

As soon as all fever was gone, the master miner got out of bed and headed for his old diggings.

3

"John Mackay is about the only friend left to the Comstock," Robert Keating asserted roundly, "and his errand to Virginia was solely to see what could be done for the people there. I do not know that he had the slightest idea that there was a possibility of renewing the Bonanza days, but he did think there was enough ore left to pay expenses and furnish work for the hundreds of old fellows who have lived their lives there, and are too set in their ways and too old to strike out for fresher fields.

"This idea ran through all his talking and planning: he wanted to help his old associates, and was willing to sacrifice his time and spend his money if he could do so. The man who shot him was either a fiend, or else he knew mighty little about John Mackay."[1]

The spontaneous homage of his friends bore witness to his honesty of intentions. His allegiance to the kingdom of quartz and clay was no posturing. It was the most stable emotion of his life.

At the hospital, Wesley C. Rippey, who failed both in murder and in suicide, was asked if Mr. Mackay had ever done him a personal injury.

"No," the pitiful old fellow answered. "Not any more than a number of the manipulators. There are hundreds of poor men in the city who have a just cause to put him out of the way. I shot him because it was time to call him to a halt. He is a bad man for the country."

Rippey's activities dated back to 1884, when he called at Flood's residence in Menlo Park, complaining that he had lost nine thousand dollars in stock—most of it in the Utah mine.

The wealthy stock operator explained that the Bonanza firm did not own Utah, that its stock was absolutely worthless, and that he couldn't sell it for him at any figure. With that, Flood gave him ten dollars and sent him away.

The embittered speculator was not so easily forgotten. On May 12, two weeks after the visit, Flood recieved a long letter from Rippey demanding restitution for the enclosed certificates of 100 shares of Utah stock, which had cost him $1,-170.

Captain Lees of the detective force, to whom the letter was handed for investigation, sought out Rippey and explained that Flood had nothing to do with the stock.

This did not terminate the affair, for on September 23 he sent the Bonanza financier another note, informing him that he had sold the shares for $37.50. With the ten dollars given him by Flood, the balance due was now $1,120.50. There followed further threats, and complaints that letters sent to Fair and Mackay had not been answered. Once again the detective warned him to keep away from the Bank of Nevada and cease his correspondence.

With age and poverty increasing, the old fellow began to rave more and more about his misfortunes. He met two men in Pauper Alley who were equally weary of life. The three formed a suicide pact.

One fulfilled his part of the agreement by jumping from the wharf. The remaining pair added a new clause to the bargain: each should take a Comstock millionaire with him. Thus it happened that John Mackay was chosen as Rippey's companion in death.

After his attempt at assassination, Rippey lay untouched in Lick Alley as hundreds of curious persons gathered about him. Both the morgue and the police were notified. The patrol wagon arrived first and the officer saw that the man was still alive, so he took him to the receiving hospital.

By a caprice of fate, Rippey's own shot cured him of a chronic case of pleurisy by clearing out the congestion, and in time he recovered. In his pocket had been found a second revolver with a fresh charge in it. Had he used this weapon instead of the one with damp shells in it, there would have been a different ending to the affair.

Simple assault was the verdict and six months in the county jail his sentence.

4

John Mackay remained in San Francisco, listening for the clapping of great machines on the Comstock, hearing only a quaver of loneliness.

In August of the same year, 1893, he was taken seriously ill at the Palace Hotel. The report was that the old bullet wound was bothering him, but Drs. Keeney and Morse diagnosed the disturbance as appendicitis.

An operation was immediately performed and the patient recovered with no difficulty. However, when the bill was presented—"$7,500 from Dr. Keeney and $5,000 from Dr. Morse, which was at the rate of about $150 a visit"—mental complications set in.

Mackay was incensed. He positively would not pay these exorbitant fees. Even when a court fight was promised him, he remained firm in his refusal. The matter hung fire for weeks, a compromise being finally arranged to the dissatisfaction of all parties concerned. The surgeons were said to have received about two-thirds of the original amount.

Eight thousand dollars still seemed outrageous to Mackay, but he had learned that when one's pockets are heavy with silver, he must expect other hands than his own within their depths.

16   The Crown is Removed

1

The shadows of John Mackay's influence continued to lengthen as the land lines auxiliary to the cable company developed and extended. Returning to New York in 1894 with health regained, he gave a banquet for the officers and chiefs of departments of both the Commercial Cable and Postal Telegraph systems in the latter's new offices. This celebration of the opening of the telegraph building on the corner of Broadway and Murray coincided with the fiftieth anniversary of the sending of the first telegraph message between Baltimore and Washington—May 24.

Of greater importance was the fact that this date marked the entrance of Clarence Mackay, age twenty, into his father's business. Shortly, this son was given voice and vote in the executive committee of both companies, and a vice-president's chair.

It was fortunate that part of the burden was shifted to his young shoulders, for a tragedy occurred the following year, on October 18, which increased the need for the younger son, and caused a complete change in the well-made plans of John Mackay.

John William, Jr., bachelor heir, twenty-six years old, was killed near the village of Mayet, France—approximately 150 miles from Paris. In the course of a race, his horse stumbled and threw him violently. He died a few hours after the accident from a fractured skull.

Mrs. Mackay withdrew from society. The father grew more silent as the clarity of his thought was blurred by the terrific loss. He had counted so much on "Willie," and this

164

son had always shown the keenest interest in his father's many enterprises.

To relieve the tension of his heavy heart, Mackay ordered a half-dozen free beds in New York hospitals to be maintained in his son's momory. Then he turned to the more careful grooming of Clarence for the duties and responsibilities of the great cable company. In work he could drown his thoughts.

2

The pattern of Mackay's life was nearly completed. One of its strongest threads came to an end on December 28, 1894, when the iron fingers in the soft glove of James Fair relaxed forever. The easy chuckles and ready answers were silenced, and the cool, hazel eyes with their expression of mock humility were closed in endless sleep.

During his six years in Washington as senator, Fair had managed to maintain that bland appearance of constant cheerfulness without family or true friends. His defeat for re-election was to be expected, for he had "but little to say in public, and was the author of very few bills."[1]

There had been no financial gain for Fair in the senatorship, but, having sold his last holdings on the lode in 1885, the lack of other interests may have prompted his desire for a second term. The capitol did not offer him, however, sufficient scope for the peculiar capacity and longheadedness of Colonel Fair. Mrs. Fair received some compensation for her long struggle for social prominence when their elder daughter, Theresa Alice, married Hermann Oelrichs of New York, and Virginia, known as "Birdie," married William K. Vanderbilt, Jr. The senatorship may have helped there.

"I don't know of any mistake that I ever made in my life—everything I have touched and everything I have reported upon has turned out just as I reported it, or as I expected. I have been fortunate in that way—it may be judgment. I never followed the ideas of anybody," were Fair's own words.[2]

However, the finger of failure made a long smudge on the portrait of the balanced, clever millionaire after his decease. The cankerous obituary, the twenty-six separate suits contesting his will, the six scandalous years required to settle his estate, indicate that his attempt to deceive others had resulted in a betrayal of himself. Like William Sharon, part of Fair's trouble came from a woman.

Her name was Mrs. Nettie R. Craven, principal of the Mission Street Grammar School in San Francisco, and she was the divorced wife of Professor Andrew Craven, principal of the Alameda High School. Claiming that Fair and she had been secretly married in Sausalito in 1892, the dynamic Mrs. Craven-Fair, as she called herself, asked for one third of his estate. The courts, however, never recognized her claims, and whether the heirs paid her $50,000, as was rumored, no one will ever know.

Fair's property at the time of his death included some 12,-000 to 14,000 acres of land throughout California, a large interest in the Pacific Rolling Mills and other factories, sixty acres of property and the Lick House in San Francisco, the million-dollar mansion in Menlo Park where his last lonely years were spent, a share in the Ohio River Railroad Company, and approximately 165,000 tons of wheat—a total of $15,000,000 instead of the estimated $40,000,000 fortune.

3

In August of 1895, John Mackay made his farewell visit to the beloved lode. The three Bonanza Kings who had ridden right and left of him were gone; but "the Boss" intended to gallop on to a dramatic finish.

Clarence Mackay's marriage on May 17, 1898, to Katherine Alexander Duer—descendant of Lady Kitty, Virginia belle of the Revolutionary era—prompted his father to make another purchase of real estate in the East.

Harbor Hills, a six-hundred-acre country estate above the little village of Roslyn, Long Island, became a quiet retreat for the aging king. In its imposing French dwelling high above Hempstead Bay, where the twenty-year-old Mrs. Mackay occupied her time with school matters, local politics, writing, and philanthropic work, and Clarence went out to make a name for himself on the turf by building up a fine stable of running horses, John Mackay formulated plans for the third and greatest step in his cable enterprise.

To bind the new Pacific possessions of the United States to the mother country was his scheme, and into this new project went all his old energy and zeal. A cable line from the Pacific coast to the Philippines, via Hawaii, without government aid or public subsidy, another link in the belt around the world for the good of commerce and to bring peace among nations—this was his present vision.

"I'll lay that Pacific cable and then retire from business," he told his friends.

Clarence would tend to it well, he knew, for he was soberminded and businesslike, lacking the ostentation expected in a son of wealth.

Mackay made other plans for the future, taking a lesson from James Fair. In December of 1900, he filed with Edmond Godchaux, recorder in San Francisco, deeds to his large lot on the southeast corner of Market and Fourth Streets, and his half interest in the Nevada Block at Montgomery and Pine Streets. James L. Flood possessed the other portions of the bank property and the Grand Opera property near Third and Mission, the latter being worth a million and a quarter.

Mackay was a large owner in the White Nob Copper Company of Mackay, Idaho, had heavy interests in the Sprague Elevator and Electrical Works of New York and the Goose Mining Company at Nome, owned the Postal Telegraph Building in New York City, was part owner of the twenty-one-story Commercial Cable Company's building there and also of some adjacent property, owned a half interest with James L. Flood in the 1,000-acre Buri Buri Rancho at San Mateo, the 1,500-acre Coleman Tract at San Rafael, and 3000 acres of timberland along the Eel River in Mendocino County, possessed several thousand acres of woodland between Reno and Truckee, California, besides a controlling interest in many enterprises of the Comstock.

The Bonanza King was president of the Mackay-Bennett Cable Company, the Postal Telegraph Company, and the prospective Pacific Commercial Cable Company, was vice-president of the new seven-million-dollar sugar refinery at Yonkers, New York (of which Gus Spreckels was president), was director of the Southern and Canadian Pacific railroads, and of the newly proposed railway from Santiago to Havana, Cuba.

His early zeal, which uncovered a great talent, had brought about productive consequences. The wings that had lifted him high still carried him forward. Not to leave a record of himself was Mackay's aim, but to expand his sway and thereby satisfy the persistent desires of that compelling inner self.

4

Once again Louisa Mackay raised her social wand to the world of fashion when she reopened magnificent Carlton House in May of 1901. During her retirement she had traveled considerably, spending a season in the Bradley Martin castle near Balmacaan, Scotland.

Her return to drawing-room affairs was handled by the impish, daring Harry Lehr, who had replaced Ward McAllister as the guiding hand of New York's social functions. Small parties and musicales were no longer popular. Lavish entertainments were both Mrs. Mackay's and Mr. Lehr's forte. London and New York were happy over her reappearance.

"With the dinner and concert given a year ago in honor of her daughter, Princess Colonna, and her son and daughter-in-law, Mr. and Mrs. Clarence Mackay, this remarkable woman, who now has the prestige of a duchess, formally reassumed her position of unquestioned supremacy," the *San Francisco Chronicle* of July 15, 1901, reported. "Not until the present summer, however, was society at liberty to count upon her as it formerly had done. And when the doors of that modern palace, 6 Carlton House Terrace, were flung open for the first social event of the present season, everybody whom Londoners consider of importance came up the famous Italian staircase, to be greeted by the small, graceful woman in black, with black pearls, whose millions are uncounted, whose disbursement of them is regal, and *whose social sway in surpassed by that of no native English woman of whatever rank.*"

The "Bonanza Queen" from Nevada was the rival of every social celebrity on the Continent, but a year from this time her black jewels would be worn in mourning. Even kings are not immortal.

5

There was no hint of disaster on Tuesday, July 15, when John Mackay saw Princess Eva off for Paris. He was apparently in excellent spirits and good health, except for some rheumatism and gout.

There were still a few arrangements for the laying of the Pacific cable to be completed. On his last visit to California he had inspected various points along the coast, and had decided upon San Francisco as the most suitable landing place for the American terminus.

Upon boarding the train for New York, around June 1, he had told Dick Dey that the first section of the new line—to Hawaii—would be in operation on Thanksgiving Day, and the remaining stretch of cable would be completed by July 1 of 1903.

After leaving his adopted daughter at the railway station, Mackay joined G. G. Ward, general manager of the Commercial Cable Company, for lunch and a discussion of business. As the two men ate their meal, Mackay was suddenly seized with a chill. Mr. Ward assisted him into a cab and sent him home to bed.

His doctors were summoned, and the trouble was diagnosed as prostration from the extreme heat of the day, with the possibility of a cold developing. The family was not told at first that his heart was very weak, since the physicians were confident that, with complete rest, there would be no cause for concern.

On Wednesday and Thursday he showed signs of improvement, but an acute turn for the worse occurred on Friday. There were symptoms of pneumonia in the left lung. Dr. Jones, Dr. Orr, and Sir Richard Douglas Powell held a consultation. There was little medical science could do except administer oxygen to assist the slowing pulse.

At six thirty on Sunday evening, July 20, the seventy-year-old master miner passed on, peacefully, without pain. At his side were his wife, Countess Telfener, and her mother, Mrs. Hungerford.

6

The carriages began to arrive at Carlton House. Though John Mackay had spent but little time in England, the innumerable cards of condolence further attested to his popularity. The Americans in the city, including General Wheeler, ex-Governor Frank Brown of Maryland, and Congressman Jefferson Levy of New York, tendered the following resolution:

"We have heard with profound regret and sorrow of the death of John William Mackay, whose eminent career is recognized as so *typical* of a high standard of American manhood, that we, in common with all Americans, desire to record our respect and regard for Mr. Mackay as a man and a citizen, and express to his family our deep sympathy for them in their bereavement."

Eva, summoned from Paris when her stepfather's condition became serious, arrived an hour after his passing. Clarence canceled his plans for the August racing season and sailed on the *Campania* for London. It was he who must return the body of his father to the family mausoleum in Brooklyn.

In 1900 the millionaire had ordered built a magnificent mausoleum near the entrance of Green-Wood Cemetery. Three hundred thousand dollars went into its contsruction. Mackay would occupy the fourth of twenty-four niches, along with Colonel Dan Hungerford, Mrs. Mackay's brother, and John William, Jr.

Across the front of the great tomb are four life-size figures of bronze: the Angel of Mercy crowning Hope, symbol of Mackay's many charities and his long list of regular pensioners; the Angel of Religion consoling Grief—he was a fervent Catholic; the Angel of Peace, peace furthered by his cable system; and the Angel of Faith arousing Youth—faith, the bulwark of his life.

As to the value of his estate, a person close to the Commercial Cable Company said, "I should think it is more than fifty million."

Life went on much as usual in the Mackay household. Eva, divorced from the count, continued as her mother's companion until September 19, 1928, when the eighty-five-year-old queen joined the departed king.

17   Echoes

1

"Death of John William Mackay Removes a Typical American," was the caption of the *New York Herald*.

"The Pacific Coast lost one of its best friends and most sterling and enterprising citizens," read the *San Francisco Chronicle*.

The world agreed that of all those who had followed the richest underground run in the world, John Mackay was the most spectacular example of earned success.

"Everybody always liked Mackay, he was so truthful," said D. O. Mills, former business enemy of the Bonanza King.

P. H. Lannan of Salt Lake City had known Mackay for forty years. This was his summary of his friend:

"His greatest traits were his unostentatious generosity and charity, and his wonderful *Americanism*. Considering the latter, it seems an irony of fate that he should have died on foreign land. His charities, I know, amounted to more than a quarter of a million a year; and so modestly were they given that no one, except his private secretary, knew the beneficiaries."[1]

Dan De Quille, the exhaustless writer of the *Territorial Enterprise* whose hobbies ranged from the ultra-scientific to harboring a band of horned toads, was one of the recipients of a pension from John Mackay. It took a very little to place a claim on the heart of the millionaire. He loved the slim, tall journalist. The power that money gave him—the power to make this old and feeble friend comfortable and return him to the Iowa farm with his long-deserted family—repaid Mackay a thousand times for the curses he had received on

171

his ambition. Upon learning of Dan De Quille's passing, he mourned with an intensity that was unashamed.

Another friend, John McCullough, laid claim to the charity of Mackay. The actor had abandoned the stage in 1884 to regain his health at Carlsbad, Germany. His insanity preceding his death in 1885 grieved the man who had worshipped him across the footlights. Mackay's contribution to the monument on the actor's grave in Mount Moriah Cemetery, Philadelphia, was perhaps the largest amount subscribed.

For many years, Mackay paid the taxes on large properties owned by Nevada's famous senator, John Percival Jones. At the time Jones was in financial difficulty, and Mackay was aware that this property—most of it in Santa Monica, California—would eventually be very valuable. General Grant shared Mackay's love for this joyous, brilliant man, who had graduated from the Comstock.

Grant, himself, felt the power of the Mackay fortune. When the general returned to New York City, following his tour of the world, he was without adequate income. George W. Jones, proprietor of the *New York Times,* proposed a permanent fund of $250,000 for the ex-president and his family, the amount to be raised by popular subscription. John Mackay, Jay Gould, and William H. Vanderbilt each donated $25,000 for this purpose, the fund being invested to provide an income of $15,000 a year.

Being anything but a businessman, Grant was delighted with the arrangement. He settled down in a red brick house, No. 3 East Sixty-sixth Street, and took over the president's chair of the Mexican Southern Railway Company. He had not smoked many cigars in this Wall Street office when scandal broke out around him and all but sent him to prison along with Ferdinand Ward, "Young Napoleon," who involved the unsuspecting soldier in swindling operations.

Following this difficult affair, the trust fund invested in railroads failed to pay the anticipated income. To augment this source of livelihood, Grant consented to write his memoirs in 1885 at the insistence of Mark Twain, chief owner of the Charles L. Webster Publishing House.

Grant's death, close to that of John McCullough, was another blow to Mackay. The Grant monument on Riverside Drive, New York City, was dedicated by President McKinley on April 27, 1897. Mackay's donation of twenty-five thousand dollars was again one of the largest contributions toward its erection. His offer to be one of ten persons to make the fund one million dollars was not accepted; few of Grant's friends were wealthy enough at the time for such a gift.

Another less-known act of kindness was related by Edmond Godchaux, who had made three trips across the Atlantic with Mackay, toured Europe with him, and corresponded with him to the last.

"Few people know how truly good a man Mackay was. He was so many-sided a man that he was seldom understood. He never sought for popularity, and he shunned publicity. He did a thousand kindly acts of charity about which people knew nothing.

"When Madam Sembrich, the prima donna, was here last, some paper printed the fact that her son was lying dangerously ill in Germany, and that she could obtain no reliable news of his condition.

"Mackay's eye caught the item while we were at dinner, and he made me stop my meal to go to Madam Sembrich and offer her the free and immediate use of the Mackay-Bennett cables. She availed herself of the privilege, and learned that her son could not recover, but she reached her son's bedside before his death."[2]

Not only persons of fame, but those in the more simple walks of life benefited by the Mackay pleasure in doing things for others. He gave large contributions for the victims of famines and floods, and the Catholic orphan asylum of some 130 children at Virginia City was supported by him.

When the Spanish-American War broke out in Cuba in 1898, he heard that there was a great need for ice for the fever patients in the American Army. Without delay, Mackay hired a steamer, ordered it to be loaded with five thousand tons of ice from the Penobscot River in Maine, and had it dispatched to the war camps.

"Mackay was a typical Western man, reticent, self-contained and modest, but full of confidence, vigor, and courage," The *San Francisco Chronicle* stated. "And above all, he was generous and kind-hearted, as hundreds who have known his bounty can testify to. The estimation in which he is held in San Francisco is shown by the comments on his death.

"Good fortune never made him arrogant, and he remained a favorite among old miners who had toiled with him on an equal plane in the days of his early struggles. For them he had always a kindly and homely word of greeting."

Richard Dey issued a statement that Mackay would have approved:

"The laying of the trans-Pacific cable Mackay considered the crowning achievement of his remarkably successful business life, but his death will not in the least interfere with its completion."[3]

Transpacific service would be effected in 1904, and the first cable between New York and Cuba completed three years later.

2

June 10, 1908, was declared a state holiday in Nevada, a day set aside by act of the legislature for the dedication of the Mackay School of Mines and of the Gutzon Borglum statue of John Mackay on the university grounds at Reno. Both were gifts to the state and the university from Mrs. Mackay and her son Clarence Mackay.

The impressive services, attended by ten thousand persons, were held before the bronze masterpiece created by the great sculptor. Clarence Mackay began his address:

When we heard of the proposal before the Legislature to erect a statue of my father as a type of the hardy pioneers who began to develop the State, both my mother and myself felt an instinctive pride, which might, I think, be considered pardonable. But we could not but feel also that there should be linked with this public recognition our own loving, personal tribute. Hence our request that we be permitted to make this presentation. . . .

It was the intention of my father during his lifetime to put in some permanent and useful form an indication of his appreciation of what Nevada had done for him. . . .

We could think of no token more certain to serve that purpose than a School of Mines, which should afford to young men facilities to acquire training and education not accessible to the youthful miners of my father's time.

The address of Mr. George Harvey contained in part:

There could not be found a finer example of the effect of opening the door to personal initiative than was embodied in John Mackay. It is difficult to recall the name of a man in whose noticeable success chance played so small a part. No advantage whatever was his, beyond that which he himself had made by rigid application to details, theoretical and practical, which gave him the mastery of his pursuit.

The lesson of John Mackay's life lies not in the wealth he acquired, but in the work he did. His was the true American spirit.

Money was but a means to an end. The millions he had won, he risked without hesitation upon a project of worldwide dimensions and of incalculable benefit to his countrymen in facilitating communication and commerce. That his great undertaking was philanthropic in the common meaning of the word, [he] himself would have been the first to deny.

There was no cautiously reasoned motive in his endeavor. It was no more or less than the instinct of a restless, rustless mind to utilize the store of energy within, in consonance with the spirit of progress which he had breathed into his lungs from the very air in which he had lived.

He had character. He never lied or cheated under any subtle pretense of any kind. The basis of his success while living, and unsullied reputation since dead, may be summed up in a single word—*integrity*.

3

All of the stories of John Mackay's life, told by men who knew him personally, re-create a portrait of a gentleman in the true sense of the word. Frowned upon, flattered, slandered, and extolled, he was never accused of those offenses which were unbecoming an understanding gentleman.

Plain, unpretending, with a genuine respect for poverty, he was a proud miner who loved art, music, and good literature; he was a simple millionaire who loved miners; he was a man who, at all times, loved ability.

To the very end, work was his trust. Through work, he had developed a warm heart, courage, and a dauntless soul. With his bluntness and strength were combined seemliness and an idealistic nature. His friends never heard him tell an unbecoming story, nor listen to an obscene tale with complacence.[4]

His mind had a spring in it, even when he was painfully in earnest. Behind his angry outbursts hovered balance and caution, and a sensitivity to impressions. Perhaps it was the ability to weigh all he heard without committing himself, to take an idea, clamp onto it with a wolf's jaw, and build it into a reality through sustained effort and not occasional bursts of enthusiasm, that was the source of his power and the secret of his accomplishments.

Highhandedness and force of will were as innate characteristics as his hidden shyness, which made him expend far greater energy than ordinary to prove to others that he was worth-while.

He followed the original trend of his nature, and few indeed were the workingmen who begrudged him his rise to fame and fortune.

"To turn back to the soil what was taken from the soil, in order that future generations may benefit in some degree by what I and mine have inherited from the soil of Nevada," was the aim of his son in his own words. The training quarters, field, stadium, and science hall are further gifts to the university from him.

Virile and strong in miner's dress stands the bronze image of John Mackay on the campus. His shirt is unbuttoned at the throat, his clay-laden trousers are tucked well into his boots. One hand grasps a pick, the other a piece of ore; but the eyes are looking far beyond the limits of his instrument. The horizon was never close to John Mackay.

It is of interest that he who was hailed as a king, as the chief of the Bonanza Kings, was selected, after death, as the most representative miner in America.

It was fitting that in the year of his death a new ore body was struck in the Con Virginia mine. The giant shaft, that daily had engulfed 75,000 cubic feet of timber hauled from the majestic forests of the Sierra Nevadas, closed rapidly thereafter, its countless cribs pressed into solid wooden cakes.

The bottom of the Comstock fissure was not reached; nor were the depths of John Mackay's nature plumbed. In some future age and civilization, those who delve deep into the humped hills of Washoe will trace the old bonanzas of silver and gold by the promising veins of lignite. Likewise, will the circles of John Mackay's influence in the pool of human memory continue to widen through the years by the waves of wireless, though the miner's voice is silenced forever.

Footnotes

CHAPTER II

1. Manuscript 55453. Supplementary notes of dictation by James G. Fair to George Howard Morrison, November 30, 1888. File of original Fair manuscripts, Bancroft Library, University of California, Berkeley, California.

2. Hubert H. Bancroft, *Chronicles of the Kings,* (San Francisco: The History Co., 1889), p. 4.

3. Manuscript 55452. Dictation by James G. Fair to George Howard Morrison, 1888. Original Fair manuscripts, Bancroft Library, p. 2.

4. *Ibid.,* p. 1.

5. Manuscript 55453. Supplementary notes of dictation by James G. Fair to George Howard Morrison, November 30, 1888. File of original Fair manuscripts, Bancroft Library, p. 23.

6. Manuscript 55452. Dictation by James G. Fair to George Howard Morrison, 1888. Original Fair manuscript, Bancroft Library, p. 5.

7. Manuscript 55453. Supplementary notes of dictation by James G. Fair to George Howard Morrison, November 30, 1888. Original Fair manuscripts, Bancroft Library, p. 2.

CHAPTER III

1. *Daily Territorial Enterprise* (Virginia City, Nevada), June 7, 1863.

CHAPTER IV

1. *San Francisco Chronicle,* July 21, 1902.

2. *San Francisco Alta,* November 3, 1866.

3. Manuscript 55452. Dictation by James G. Fair to George Howard Morrison, 1888. Original Fair manuscripts, Bancroft Library, p. 8.

4. C. C. Goodwin, *As I Remember Them* (Salt Lake City: Salt Lake Commercial Club, 1913), p. 162.

5. *Ibid.*

6. *Ibid.*

7. *Ibid.*

8. Manuscript 55452. Dedication by James G. Fair to George Howard Morrison, 1888. Original Fair manuscripts, Bancroft Library, p. 7.

CHAPTER V

1. Manuscript 55452. Dictation by James G. Fair to George Howard Morrison, 1888. Original Fair manuscripts, Bancroft Library, p. 8.

2. *Ibid.*

3. Manuscript 55451. Letter to H. H. Bancroft. Original Fair manuscripts, Bancroft Library, p. 1.

4. *San Francisco Mail,* February 21, 1877.

5. Manuscript 55451. Letter to H. H. Bancroft. Original Fair manuscripts, Bancroft Library, p. 3.

6. William Wright (Dan De Quille, pseud.) *The Big Bonanza* (New York: Alfred A. Knopf, Inc., 1947), p. 400.

7. *San Francisco Alta,* December 26, 1874.

CHAPTER VI

1. *Daily Territorial Enterprise.*

2. *Ibid.*

3. *Gold Hill* (Nev.) *News*, April 12, 1878.

4. *Ibid.*, February 26, 1881.

5. Eliot Lord, "The Mackay Memorial Statue," *World's Work*, XIII (Nov. 1906—April 1907), p. 8161.

6. *San Francisco Chronicle*, February 24, 1877.

CHAPTER VII

1. C. C. Goodwin, *As I Remember Them*, p. 161.

CHAPTER VIII

1. *San Francisco Chronicle*, April 28, 1879.

CHAPTER IX

1. *Gold Hill News*, October 25, 1876.

2. *San Francisco Chronicle*, February 24, 1879.

3. *Ibid.*

CHAPTER X

1. *San Francisco Bulletin*, May 25, 1878.

2. *San Francisco Alta*, January 11, 1877.

3. *Gold Hill News*, March 28, 1877.

4. *San Francisco Post*, February 12, 1880.

5. *Gold Hill News*, February 21, 1878.

6. *Ibid.*, June 19, 1878.

7. *San Francisco Call*, May 11, 1879.

8. *Ibid.*, June 10, 1878.

CHAPTER XI

1. *San Francisco Chronicle,* February 13, 1879.

2. *San Francisco Call,* May 15, 1879.

3. *Ibid.*

4. Eliot Lord, "The Mackay Memorial Statue," *World's Work,* XIII (Nov. 1906—April 1907), p. 8160.

5. Manuscript 55451. Letter to H. H. Bancroft. Original Fair manuscripts, Bancroft Library, p. 3.

6. *Gold Hill News,* August 20, 1880.

CHAPTER XII

1. Manuscript 55453. Supplementary notes of dictation by James G. Fair to George Howard Morrison, November 30, 1888. Original Fair manuscripts, Bancroft Library, p. 13.

2. *Gold Hill News,* December 4, 1880.

3. *Ibid.,* September 28, 1880.

CHAPTER XIV

1. *San Francisco Chronicle,* February 28, 1891.

2. *World-Telegram,* March 29, 1898.

3. *San Francisco Chronicle,* May 4, 1885.

4. Manuscript 55451. Letter to H. H. Bancroft. Original Fair manuscripts, Bancroft Library, p. 5.

5. C. C. Goodwin, *As I Remember Them,* p. 167.

6. *Ibid.,* p. 168.

7. Manuscript 55453. Supplementary notes of dictation by James G. Fair to George Howard Morrison, November 30, 1888. Original Fair manuscripts, Bancroft Library, p. 20.

8. Goodwin, *op. cit.,* p. 168.

9. Manuscript 55453. Supplementary notes of dictation by James G. Fair to George Howard Morrison, November 30, 1888. Original Fair manuscripts, Bancroft Library, p. 16.

10. *Ibid.*

11. Manuscript 55451. Letter to H. H. Bancroft. Original Fair manuscripts, Bancroft Library, p. 3.

12. *Ibid.*, p. 6.

13. Manuscript 55453. Supplementary notes of dictation by James G. Fair to George Howard Morrison, November 30, 1888. Original Fair manuscripts, Bancroft Library, pp. 18-19.

14. Manuscript 55452. Dictation by James G. Fair to George Howard Morrison, September 27, 1888. Original Fair manuscripts, Bancroft Library, p. 16.

15. Goodwin, *op. cit.*, p. 168.

CHAPTER XV

1. *San Francisco Chronicle,* February 25, 1893.

2. *Ibid.*, July 21, 1902.

CHAPTER XVI

1. Manuscript 55451. Letter to H. H. Bancroft. Original Fair manuscripts, Bancroft Library, p. 6.

2. Manuscript 55452. Dictation by James G. Fair to George Howard Morrison, September 27, 1888. Original Fair manuscripts, Bancroft Library, p. 21.

CHAPTER XVII

1. *New York Herald,* July 21, 1902.

2. *San Francisco Chronicle,* July 21, 1902.

3. *Ibid.*

4. R. L. Fulton, "Reminiscences," *Nevada State Historical Society Papers* (Carson City, Nev.: State Printing Office, 1908), 1907-08, p. 85.